CU00842806

First published by Serious Businessw[c]

For distributor details and how to ord[e]
www.thegirlsmeanbusiness.com/book[s]

Print ISBN: 978-1515169086

This book is dedicated to Chloe, my future little girl who means business.

Thanks to my hubby Anton, my lovely mum and Emma Holmes, my business manager who keeps everything running smoothly. Thanks too, to you and all the amazing women business owners at The Girls Mean Business around the world who keep inspiring me every day.

BONUS FREEBIES
I've put together some lovely freebie bonuses for you because you've bought this book. You can download them all here www.bitly.com/sosbizbook

Cover Design: Katherine Reynolds
Book Design: Kathy Reed

www.thegirlsmeanbusiness.com
www.facebook.com/thegirlsmeanbusiness

BUSINESS MUM'S SURVIVAL GUIDE FOR THE SCHOOL HOLIDAYS

CONTENTS

INTRODUCTION

The thing about school holidays is that everything changes. Your routine goes out the window and it's easy to kid yourself that you'll be able to muddle through but often (usually on the first Wednesday of the first week of the holidays) reality bites and you find yourself tearing your hair out and wondering how on earth you are going to get through the next few weeks.

Having survived quite a few school holidays and because I deal with thousands of women business owners through The Girls Mean Business every month, I've gathered a big stash of tips and tactics that will help you survive the school holidays with your business and sanity intact.

This is meant to be a
'pick it up when you need it' kind of book, a
'stick it in your handbag when you're out and about' kind of book, a
'grab a tip to get me by' kind of book.

It's a quick reference book to help you out when you really need it, to give you ideas and shortcuts. It's designed to be flung in your rucksack or suitcase, left in the car to read while you're waiting for soccer class to finish or left in the kitchen if you've just grabbed enough time to make a cuppa.

It's designed for you if you love your kids more than life itself but the thought of NOT working on your business all school holidays would drive you (and them) insane. I'm there with you, lovely lady.
I'm a mum of a seven-year-old daughter. I've managed to build a pretty big online business while bringing up Chloe and dealing with her ever-expanding social and extra-curricular life, along with her developing attitude (yikes!). I definitely feel like I'm having a premonition of the teenage years and it's not pretty!

I know what it's like to feel under pressure to keep the business going despite needing (and wanting) to spend time with the family. I know what it's like to be working until the early hours because you're off on holiday in the morning and you're nowhere near finished what you needed to do.

This book isn't for you if

- you've got this 'school holiday / business thing' cracked.
- It's not for you if you're cool about taking the whole time off to be with the children.
- It's not for you if you are already a super-business ninja whose business runs beautifully on autopilot.

This book IS for you if:

- You're a business-owner mum of school age children and the thought of the school holidays is inducing worry and panic
- You're doing OK but it would GREAT to get some tips and advice to add to your armoury
- You're wondering, quite frankly how on earth you manage to run a business at the best of times, let alone in the school holidays. It's a dark art you don't feel you've mastered and you need all the help you can get.

Breathe easy, lovely lady. I can help.
This book isn't the answer to life, the Universe and everything but it WILL help you make the most of the school holidays, keep the children happy, keep your business running healthily and giving YOU some time for you, too.

Keep reading, I think you're going to like this!

Love, Claire xx

SUPER CUSTOMER

Before we get stuck into the business and marketing stuff, let me just share my biggest trade secret with you. It's what I teach ALL my clients from day one and when they get it, it works like MAGIC!

Let's talk Super Customers because they are going to change the way you look at marketing forever. Nobody teaches us this, we don't get taught it in school or on most business courses, it kind of gets skipped over in the 'target market' section. But it deserves more attention than that because once you understand who your Super Customer is, your marketing will be:

- Easier
- Quicker
- More Effective

You'll not waste time on marketing that doesn't work and you'll never be stuck for words – you'll always know what you need to say in your blogs, e-newsletters and Social Media posts.

It's like a best-kept secret but once you know it, it changes the way you market your business forever. It's clever marketing.

WHY IS SUPER CUSTOMER MARKETING SO AWESOME?

Well, you are a micro-business owner and mum, like me. You have a business to run and a family to look after so you have limited time, money and energy to spend on marketing.

You want to focus your limited time, money and energy on marketing that is most likely to work.

Super customer marketing means that you can get SUPER focused on the people who are MOST LIKELY TO BUY from you, instead of trying to please and attract everybody.

Super customer marketing you don't waste time and money and energy on marketing that will never work.

Super Customer marketing is more efficient and more effective. It's much quicker to decide upon and implement. Once you understand super customer marketing, you will never go back.

HOW WILL I KNOW WHO MY SUPER CUSTOMER IS?

Do you have any customers in your business who are a joy to work with? You know what I mean:

- The time flies when you are with them
- They are a joy to work with
- They never complain
- They feel like a perfect fit for your business
- They think you are a genius, a miracle worker or both
- They keep coming back
- They tell all their friends
- They never quibble on price
- They love everything you do
- They really value you
- You find it easy to help them

It may be that not one single customer fits this profile by themselves, but you might have several customers who all fit certain criteria and whom, if you put them together like a photo fit picture, would create a super customer profile.

Ideally, your super customers hang out together in groups too, so you can easily get in front of lots of them are the same time.

And finally, they need to have the money to be able to afford you.

This is important.

It's not enough to like you and value you, they have to have the means to pay you and be willing to invest in what you sell.

I say this because I get a lot of ladies who want to deal with people who have very little money. This is lovely but you can't build a business selling to people who have no money unless they get funding grants from other sources.

What I often suggest is that you build a business based on people who can and will pay for you, and who do value you, and when you have got your business expenses covered and you have a decent salary and savings in place you can choose to setup regular payments to a charity or do some pro bono work.

THE BAD CUSTOMER APPROACH

If you're still struggling to think who your super customer might be, try looking at it in a different way.

Think about your worst customers.

Think about all the bad customers you've ever had in your business. Are you shuddering already? Good! Now think about what it was about them that made them such a bad fit for you and your business.

- Was it the fact that they kept haggling over price?
- What is the fact that you could never please them and they were never satisfied, however much you tried?
- What are the fact that the brief kept changing and the goalposts kept moving as soon as you thought you were on track?
- Was it the fact that it just felt like hard work when you were with them?

Whatever the reasons, and you will know what they are, the people we're describing now are the opposite of whom you want to attract.
So why not start there?

Why not make list of all the attributes and characteristics that you DON'T want in your super customer and then you can work out what you do want – the opposite!

Notes

WHY IS YOUR SUPER CUSTOMER SO IMPORTANT?

So, why is your super customer so important? Why are we going to all this trouble to identify this Super Customer for your business?

Well, remember you don't have the time money or energy to market to everybody because you are a micro business owner.

You may as well use your limited resources to market to the people who are most likely to buy from you – your super customers.

And now we know they are, we can start to speak their language. Speak to them in a way that resonates with them, because it touches on their issues and their struggles and shows how you can help them.

Let me give you an example:

My super customers are women business owners and female entrepreneurs who are struggling with time, marketing, productivity, confidence, and running a business while raising a family or managing other responsibilities.

I talk to them in my marketing.

I ask questions like:

- 'Are you struggling with your marketing?',
- 'Do you wish you had more hours in the day?',
- 'Are you trying to run your business while raising a family/holding down a job?',
- 'Do you wish you could get more sales and more customers and build your business, and still have a life?'

When I ask questions like this in my marketing, my Super Customers are nodding their heads to themselves. They are recognising themselves in my description because I've touched on issues they're struggling with.

You've Been Super-Customered!

I'm sure it's happened to you when you've read a piece in a magazine, or a sales page, when it feels like it's speaking to you - as though the author knows you really well? As if they're a mind-reader?

When that happens to us we often buy because the product or service is such a good fit. When that happens you know you're probably their Super Customer.

And you can do the same for your Super Customers in your marketing.

Knowing about Super Customers is going to radically reduce the amount of time, money and energy you are wasting in your business because all of your marketing from now on will be targeted at people who are a really good fit.

During the school holidays, this is more important than ever because, frankly, time is in short supply with the kids around, so you need to make every marketing minute count. And Super Customer marketing is how you'll do that.

Not only that, but you'll get better results from your marketing.

So, let's just get clear – you're spending LESS time on marketing but you're getting BETTER results...what's not to love?

'Your Super Customer'
by Chloe Mitchell (7)

WORK OUT YOUR SUPER CUSTOMER

Get a notebook and pen (or scribble in this book, that's what it's for!), grab a cuppa and start working out who your Super Customer could be. Don't worry if you can't quite crack it straight away, it will come over time and the more of your Super Customers you attract, the more you will find out about them and the more targeted you can be.

Figuring out your Super Customer might be the most important thing you ever do for your business – either way, you're going to find your marketing a zillion times easier and that's got to be a good thing.

TIME – SAVING IT, FINDING IT AND DOING MORE WITH IT

During school holidays, time is the thing we miss the most. Our term-time routine goes out the window and we have to try to keep our business running in a fraction of the time we usually have.

The first thing you need to realise is that you CAN keep your business running but you're going to have to compromise and use workarounds. You can't realistically fit in everything you usually get done when you have full, uninterrupted work days. If you're like me, you can pretty much work from 9- 2 between the school runs – that's a BIG chunk of time each day and during school holidays it's reduced down to an hour here and there, if you're lucky.

Keeping your business running during the school holidays means you need to prioritise, focus and stop wasting time. And if you get into those habits, your term-time working days will be way more productive too.

HOLIDAY TIME

GOING AWAY ON HOLIDAY

Let's get something straight. You are allowed time off. You don't need to apologise, fret or panic. Every business owner needs time off, or they burn out. And, you are not just any business owner, you're a mum too and you've got the kids off school for days or weeks at a time.

MANAGING CUSTOMER EXPECTATIONS

There is a big difference between dealing with a huge brand and dealing with a micro business, which is what you and I run. We don't have huge teams of staff – we are deliberately and beautifully small.

When customers buy from micro-businesses they understand that the business consists of one or two people, so when they see a holiday notice on your website and social media, they don't think badly of it. It just means that they, and you, need to plan ahead. The only people you will lose are those who want last-minute-panic orders but to be honest, you would probably struggle with those during term time anyway.

Here are some tips to help you manage customer expectations if you're going away:

1. Give people plenty of notice – depending on your business, between 6 and 4 weeks is about right. Send them an email letting your customers know you're not around for a couple of weeks (remind them closer to the time too)
2. Put notifications on your social media and website
3. Put an auto responder on your email
4. Let people know when they can expect to hear from you

5. When you return, let people know you are back
6. Don't forget to take off your 'holiday' notification on your social media, website and email auto responder

HOLIDAY HOURS

Whether or not you're going away, the rest of the time you're still on restricted hours if you have the kids around. It's up to you how you handle customer expectations during this time but if you're expecting lots of enquiries then it's best to let people know the situation so they can expect a slower response and work around it.

Just like the 'I'm away for 2 weeks' tasks above, you can let people know in advance you're on reduced hours for a few weeks. Put your working days/hours on your website and social media, set up an auto responder, etc. Your Super Customers won't mind – they buy from you because they love YOU and they understand you need to work around the kids and have time off.

It's much better to be up front and transparent with your customers than try and fail to muddle through, and let them down in the process.

MANAGING WORKLOAD

If you know you're going to be away or working reduced hours, make sure you plan for this in advance. Work out how much time you are realistically going to have – and I mean REALISTICALLY.

This means that you might have to turn work away. I know. How scary is that? But how much worse would you feel if you said 'yes', took it on and then didn't have time to do it?

Life has a habit of taking over in the school holidays. I remember one year I had a week scheduled when my mum had taken Chloe away on holiday and everything depended on this particular week - I had set aside this week to record a new programme – then I lost my voice. And I couldn't do any of the work I had planned. Another time I had my childcare totally sorted for a week out of the big summer holidays and then Chloe got a bug and had to be home with me, throwing up everywhere!

This is why you need to be realistic. And also why you need to have some contingency time built in, in case something like that happens. It's much better to find yourself with unexpected free time than feel like you're fire-fighting for the entire holiday – it will cause upset with your family and will mean you are on edge the whole time, just trying and failing to get caught up.

MANAGING MARKETING

It's really important to keep your marketing going throughout the school holidays, even if you know you can't take on any extra work. You need to stay top of mind and this means keeping your marketing on drip feed all the time, even if you just trickle out the marketing over the school holidays and ramp it up once the kids are back.

You need to plan ahead as best you can, schedule in your social media, your e-newsletters, your blogs, keep adding value and showing your super customers that you're still around and still available to help them if they need you. I'm going to talk more about this later in the book.

MAKING TIME

However frazzled you're feeling during the school holidays, there's a really good chance you can create some extra time to work on your business.

Let's look at where you might be frittering away time in your business (because we all do it) and how you can create work time out of time you're wasting.

WAITING TIME

How often do you find yourself sitting around waiting for the kids – in the car? At activities and clubs? At soft play? I'm talking about those times when you're not WITH the children, other people are looking after them or they are away playing happily but you need to be there? I call this **Combo Time** and I've got loads of suggestions about exploring how to use it best.

MINDLESS TIME

How often do you find yourself aimlessly scrolling through social media for the sake of it? Or glued to a TV programme out of habit? Remember, this is school holiday business survival time so you're going to have to find time wherever you can, to make up for the work time you're losing elsewhere. You could be using this to do marketing, to plan out your cashflow, to set goals and targets, there are loads of things you can do while you're relaxing.

I get that it can be late at night before you get any 'me time' and the last thing you might feel like doing is working, and that's fine. I'm talking about evenings when you've got the kids to bed and you're feeling OK and you might slip into watching the Soaps out of habit, but you can use that time much more productively.

See how you can use your MINDLESS TIME better, even if it's just for a few hours during the school holidays. Why not stick in your earphones and listen to some podcasts so you can learn while you relax? Why not sit and scope out social media posts? Or blog ideas? Or come up with the topics for your next few monthly e-newsletters?

PROCRASTINATING

Or in other words, putting stuff off. This can be a HUGE time waster because you think you're busy but actually you're just doing 'stuff' to put off doing what you need to be doing. In my case, I even have a certain thing I do when I'm procrastinating so I always know when I'm avoiding doing something important.

My procrastination behaviour is to make memes – memes are those images I use on social media, a photo or image with a quote or saying on it – like this one. When I find myself busy making memes I know I've slipped into it because I'm putting off doing something else. You need to catch yourself in the act!

What do YOU do when you're putting something else off?

Watch your behaviour over the next few days and see what you do when you're putting something off. It might be to head onto Facebook or start sorting out your emails - try to figure out what it is so you can recognise it and stop yourself doing it when you have more important things to do

FAFFING

Faffing is unproductive busy-ness and we're really good at it. Whether it's spending time on social media, doing endless 'research', starting but never finishing blogs, e-newsletters or videos – the fact is you're not achieving anything by it. You're spending time pretending to be busy but don't have anything productive to come out of it.

If you're wasting time faffing, then stop! It's not a good use of time any time of year and especially not during school holidays when you're struggling for time.

CHUNKS OF TIME

The best way to get stuff done during school holidays is to give up the idea of full working days and instead, look for chunks of time. From 10 minutes to an hour here and there, it's amazing what you can get done when you set your mind to it.

The trick is to be ready.

To have a list of jobs you can tackle, no matter how small the time slot available. It's so frustrating when you find yourself with time you could have spent on your business, just to find that you haven't a clue what to do. And the best way to do this is to have a 10 Minute List.

Let me show you how that works.

BRAIN DUMP

This is a great thing to do when you've got a head full of 'stuff' and no structure (and by the way if you're feeling like that then you're probably also feeling overwhelmed and a bit twitchy, so let's do something about it).

Have you ever been working on your computer and an error message comes up saying you're out of memory? It's when your computer is so full of stuff that it doesn't have any space left to let you process anything? – your brain is the same. You always need to leave space for processing.

This is what you need to do:

1. Get a BIG piece of paper and a pen
2. Start writing!
3. Empty your head of everything that's taking up space there
4. Keep writing until you're done

When you're writing, make sure you jot it all down, no matter how silly or irrelevant. The fact is, silly or not, these thoughts are taking up valuable space in your head and you can use that space much better. Whether it's a niggling doubt about whether you sent an email the other day, an urgent idea that you're overdue a dentist appointment, a fleeting thought that you need to invite your child's friend over for a play date, get them all out.

In among them there will be genuine work tasks that need sorting and seeing to. But you can't see them to deal with them because they are mixed in among a whole load of 'noise'.

What you're doing is emptying your brain to see what's in there, getting rid of the irrelevant stuff, dealing with the relevant stuff and leaving room for you to process it.

Keep writing and writing until you've emptied your head. Then you can applythe 3D approach.

DITCH
DELEGATE
DO (or Schedule)

DITCH

Go through and get rid of all the out-dated, irrelevant thoughts that are cluttering up your brain, and there WILL be some. With me when I do this, I always have thoughts in there that I've already dealt with (I know, that sounds so weird) but here's an example. I'll have a persistent, niggly thought that I want to try a certain piece of software but maybe my team and I have already decided against it for a good reason, yet the original thought is still in there. I can get rid of it, it's dealt with. Get ditching!

DELEGATE

Then go through all the other thoughts and tasks and see what you can delegate or outsource. Maybe you've got 'tidy kids' rooms' or 'do ironing' on your list. Can you ask the kids to tidy their own rooms? Even if it's just to put their washing in a basket? Can you ask someone else to do the ironing? And if that thought seems like an impossible dream, remember this is School Holiday Survival mode and a few weeks of bedroom chaos and crumpled clothes aren't going to kill anyone. Maybe you just need to let them go till the schools go back. Either way, get them out of your head.

If it's work stuff like 'set up email newsletter template' then why not hire a Virtual Assistant for an hour? A good V.A can whip up a simple branded e-newsletter template in that time and it might have cost you £20/$30. Well worth the money to get it off your list and let you start using it.

DO (OR SCHEDULE) IT

This is where you make sense of all that's left. Some you'll be able to do now and others you'll be able to schedule into your calendar to do later – but you know they're covered and you'll think about them when that scheduled time comes up in your diary.

BIG JOBS DON'T EXIST

Some things on your To Do list will be small but others will be HUGE and you'll never feel that you have enough time to tackle them.
I have a little trick for you. **Let me explain:**

You know what it's like, you write your To Do list and you find that most of the jobs have been on there forever. There's never enough time in the day to even start them, let alone finish them and you'd need to book in 2 weeks of dedicated time just for them, to have a fighting chance of getting them done. Except it's the school holidays and any time you book in is either family holiday time (in other words, NO working) or it's time with the children which means it's not your most productive time ever.

What you need to do is NEVER have huge jobs on your list, then you'll never feel stuck! Easy!

OK, let me tell you how that works in real life.

If you have jobs on your list like 'update my website' or 'start blogging' or 'set up a podcast' or 'do an e-newsletter' they all feel like BIG jobs. You can't just sit down with a cup of tea for 10 minutes and do one of those from start to finish.

This means you get stuck. You're paralysed into inaction because everything feels too big and scary to start. What you need is to break every big job down. And then break it down again. And then break it down again because most jobs are a series of smaller tasks that can be done independently. If you keep breaking down every big job as far as you can, you'll be left with a 10 minute list. And making a 10 minute list is how I start most days.

10 MINUTE LIST

Every morning during term time, pretty much, I get Chloe off onto the school bus and I'm back at the house by 8am. I grab a cup of my favourite Early Grey tea and my notepad and I start writing. I do a mini brain dump and write down all the jobs I need to do. And then I break down any big jobs into smaller jobs, and so on until I have a big list of little tasks.

And those little tasks are the perfect size for me to do in 10 minute chunks of time. They include things like 'make dentist's appointment' or 'decide on topic for next week's newsletter' or 'respond to Twitter comments' or 'ask a question on my Facebook page'. Nothing big, nothing onerous.

The BIG jobs like 'update my website' have been broken down into little tasks, so that one might look like this:

- Make a list of pages that need updating (10 mins)
- Scope out new wording for each page (10 mins per page)
- Write a paragraph at a time till updates are complete (10 mins per paragraph)
- Find images for front page (10 mins per image)
- Email photographer to get photo for 'about' page sorted (10 mins)
- Come up with idea for Irresistible Freebie (10 mins)
- Scope out Irresistible Freebie (10 mins)
- Write/record Irresistible Freebie (however long this one takes, but break it down)

Do you get the idea? Virtually every big job can be broken down into far more manageable tasks that you can fit in and around other stuff. Which is perfect for the school holidays but works all the time for me.

BACK POCKET LIST

I take this a step further. Because I live in Jeans and slouchy trousers, I always have a handy pocket but a handbag would do just as well. Once I've got my 10 minute list I complete and tick off as many of the little jobs as I can before I head out – this works brilliantly during school holidays because we're rarely stuck at home. Once we get to the park, or soft play, or to gymnastics practise or drama bootcamp, if I have to wait for Chloe I dig out my 10 minute list and off I go.

I've always got my phone with me and I usually take my iPad as part of my 'Work From Anywhere Kit', along with my notebook and a pen – that's pretty much everything I need. I make phone calls, I write emails, I scope out blogs (I have a scope-a-blog template I use for that one), I respond to comments on my social media accounts, I brainstorm ideas for books or blogs or e-newsletters. I make every minute count. I also keep an eye on what Chloe's doing but I know she'll shout for me if she needs me.

My 10 minute list means none of the tasks need my attention for long – I just need to get stuck in and tick them off, one by one. And that's a great feeling – coming back from a day out with Chloe when I've spent time with her and she's been doing something she loves AND I've piled through my 10 minute list and got loads done.

Result! And the perfect example of Combo time, which I'll tell you more about shortly.

DOING MORE WITH YOUR TIME

Not all time during School Holidays is family time or Combo time; sometimes you'll also get full-on proper work time (yay!).

My mum always takes Chloe away for a week in our caravan during our long school holidays and I get TONS done. My husband is usually working because he saves his vacation time for our family holidays together, so I'm by myself, just me and Meg the puppy, and I can crack on.

Because I know weeks like this are a rare and precious thing and I can work till midnight if I like. This is something I can never do during term time because we're up at 6 and out the door at 7.30 and something I can't do when Chloe is around because her bedtime is a 2 hour challenge that leaves me emotionally sapped and physically drained (love her to bits but wish she'd just go to sleep when she needs to!) I really REALLY make the most of them. Other than unforeseen challenges like losing my voice when I've set that week aside to record a programme, I can power through jobs like Wonder Woman.

I use a few little tricks to make sure every bit of work time counts, whether I've got a week or just a couple of hours while Chloe is at my sister's for the afternoon.

FOCUS

The first thing to do when you get rare and precious full-on work time is to get focused, quickly. It's so easy to make a cuppa, spend time on Facebook, browse the stationery on Amazon and before you know it, an hour has vanished into thin air. Eeek! You can't afford that to happen.

Here are 6 tips to help you get focused when you're feeling all over the place.

1. STOP MULTI-TASKING

It's common knowledge that women are brilliant at multi-tasking, and we are. Like you, I too held a baby in my arm whilst stirring soup and changing a dentist appointment with a phone at my ear. We can all do it, but that doesn't mean we should.

In business it's a really bad idea, especially when you're trying to get something important done. So when you need to focus, stop multi-tasking and focus on ONE THING until it's done.

Close down your social media messengers and notifications, put your phone on silent and turn it over until you're done. Pick the ONE THING you're going to focus on and go for it, and don't stop until you're finished. Put everything else to the back of your mind. Everything else can wait. You will amaze yourself with how much you can get done when you're not spreading your attention across loads of different tasks.

2. FINISH THINGS THAT ARE EASILY COMPLETED

Picture the scene: You've started 4 emails to people but because you're not quite sure how to word them, they are still all open on your screen waiting for inspiration to hit you but you could easily finish them if you just gave them a bit of attention.

You almost finished that really important invoice but you needed to grab one last bit of information and you got distracted while you were looking.

Does this sound familiar? If so, then stop! Pick one of the easy jobs that is waiting half-done and finish it. Then pick another, and finish it.

They do not have to be perfect. Just get them done and out there, off your desk and out of your head. Half-finished jobs are the enemy of focus and they take up valuable mental bandwidth for no reason.

The more half-finished jobs you can get completed, the more time and space you've got to focus on the things that really matter.

3. STAY IN THE NOW

If your mind is constantly wandering off to 'I wonder what I can put in tomorrow's picnic' or 'I wonder who that woman is who put that nasty comment on my Facebook page' then you're never going to get much done.

Get into the habit of recognising when your mind is wandering and stop it mid-wander – write down the thing that was distracting you (I have an 'idea park' on the inside back cover of my notebook for just that purpose) but do nothing about it until you've finished what you're working on. Your brain loves to daydream and wander and you can lose loads of valuable time while it does it – in the school holidays you just don't have time for that. Stay in the present, focus on the task in hand and get it finished.

4. RESPONDING RATHER THAN REACTING

It's really easy to waste time dealing with instant messages, Facebook messages, texts and we're used to responding to them straight away.

Here's a thought:

They can wait.

Until you're ready.

You don't have to react right away.

Especially during the school holidays when time is of the essence, you need to stop reacting and start getting some structure in your business. It's OK to sit on an email for a couple of days, especially if you have your holiday 'working hours' list on your website and social media and an auto responder on your email. It's OK to reply when it's a good time for you, instead of immediately.

It's very rare that something is so urgent that it needs an answer now. I understand that we're in an age where people expect an instant reply. Just because you're online doesn't mean you have to reply right now. Knee-jerk reactions are the enemy of focus and during the school holidays you are going to be the QUEEN of focus. Stop reacting. Start responding when you're ready.

5. DE-CLUTTER YOUR WORKSPACE

If you are surrounded by piles of half-eaten sandwiches, paper work, magazines you were going to read later, kids' stuff waiting to be put away – how are you supposed to focus? It's not conducive to a productive work blast. Spend 10 minutes sorting it out and restoring calm to your workspace. Then crack on.

6. SET A TIMER!

If you really need to get something done and you keep getting distracted set yourself a timer on your phone or computer. Give yourself a limit of 10, 20 or 30 minutes and focus on one job for that period of time until the buzzer goes.

It's amazing how much you can get done when you're up against a deadline.

Half the reason why we allow ourselves to let tasks spread out and we don't finish them is because we're just not focussed and we've not got that urgency. Set a timer, blast through your task till you're done and then, if you're still buzzing, set another timer. It's a great psychological trick that will tap into your subconscious and bring out your competitive streak – there's nothing like a deadline to get rid of writer's block and get your creative juices flowing.

PRIORITISE

Not every job on your to do list is equally important or urgent. And not every job needs doing while the kids are off school.

The trick is working out which are important, which are urgent and which are both – and making/finding time to get them done, while putting stuff off that can be put off until the kids are back at school – why make it hard for yourself?

Look at your To Do list.

What can wait? (hint, if it's been on there a while then another few weeks won't hurt)

Apply the 3DS – can you ditch anything? Delegate anything? Schedule stuff in for later?

Does it add value? Ask yourself these questions:
- Why are you doing it?
- How is it going to add value to your business?
- Will it drive more sales?
- Make your marketing more effective? Save you tons of time and energy?

If not, why is it on your list?

SIMPLIFY

What are you overthinking? What are you over-complicating? Are you trying to reinvent the wheel all the time? What can you re-use? What can you short cut without compromising on quality or letting customers down?
Look at what's on your to do list and see if there's an easier way to accomplish the same thing.

OUTSOURCE

You don't have to do it all yourself. In fact, you shouldn't do it all yourself, even if you could. Not every task is a good use of your time.

Just because I can do basic design jobs on Canva doesn't mean I should. I can easily waste an hour on Canva and achieve an OK image, whereas if I outsourced it to my designer I'd have an AMAZING image and I'd have freed up an hour to work on what I'm good at.

Look at where you add value in your business. Look at what ONLY YOU can do - make a list! And be truthful with yourself. Instead of thinking 'oh, yes someone else could do that but it would take me so long to show them that it's not worth it', still make that list AS IF you could find the right person. You might surprise yourself and by setting your intention to find someone, you'll be amazed how often that perfect someone turns up.

- Where are you wasting time, battling with jobs that are not a good fit for you?
- What are you doing, that other people could do as well as or better than you?
- What keeps getting pushed to the back of your desk or the bottom of your to do list?

Did you know, I outsourced jobs to a virtual assistant before I could pay myself in the early days? I did it because I was working around a toddler and my time and my brain were full – I had no mental bandwidth to process anything, no time to THINK. I knew that I was stuck and that I'd stay stuck unless I could free up some thinking and processing time and the best way for me to do that was to find a virtual assistant to take on a few jobs that were holding me back.

WHAT CAN YOU OUTSOURCE?

In my case it was setting up sales forecast spreadsheets, setting up an e-newsletter template, importing my lists into Mailchimp, things that were important and needed doing but I simply didn't have the capacity to do them.

Once my virtual assistant had set them up for me, and by the way it took her about 2 hours after having been on my to do list for MONTHS, I could start sending e-newsletters, I could put my targets in place and track my sales, I could forecast my money for the next few months to stop me panicking.

These were BIGGIES and I needed someone else to intervene and help me. At the time I couldn't afford help but I also couldn't afford NOT to.

Since then, I've always outsourced – not always the same things but I have a trusted dream team to fall back on that I've built up over the years, who can step in as and when I need them.

- What can you outsource today?
  (Download my 45 things you can outsource in your business checklist for free, www.bitly.com/sosbizbook)
- What jobs are on your list that keep getting pushed back?
- What jobs are on your list that someone else could quickly and easily do for a modest investment?

Get on and outsource, free up that mental bandwidth and focus on the jobs that add value in your business.

WORK SMARTER

Working smarter is the name of the game in the school holidays. As you've seen in this chapter, it's about understanding what you're working with, getting rid of stuff you don't need to do and making the most of the time you DO have to achieve as much as possible with it.

SUPER CUSTOMER MARKETING

In the introduction we looked at your Super Customer and why you need to focus on them – that is SMART marketing and it's something that most business owners don't know so you have a secret weapon. Focusing all your marketing on your Super Customer takes bravery and a particularly large pair of big girl knickers, because your instinct will be to market far and wide and get your message out to as many people as possible. Also, everyone you meet at networking meetings will tell you you're doing it wrong and missing out on customers. But you know better.

Remember, you are a micro business owner.

You have limited time, money and energy to spend on marketing

You might as well market to the people who are most likely to buy from you – your Super Customers

By default, if you're NOT marketing to your Super Customers, you must be marketing to people who are not likely to buy. What a waste!

Super Customer Marketing is smart marketing. It focuses your time, attention, money and energy on people who are a great fit for your business. Nothing is wasted. It's an efficient, effective way of marketing.

Remember, too – you're not sacking customers (unless you want to) you can sell to whomever you wish. That's your prerogative as a business owner. You just can't MARKET to everyone.

Super Customer marketing is a business survival tool for the school holidays AND all year round.

AUTOMATE

Look at what you can automate in your business. Whether it's systems and processes or parts of your marketing, where can you use tools and technology to take YOU out of the equation, free up your precious time when you need it most and make sure things happen every time, as they ought?

Things you could automate or schedule in advance:

E-newsletters

Blogs

Facebook posts

Tweets

Customer service emails (answers to 'Frequently Asked Questions' sent out automatically when someone emails your customer service email can cut down on customer response time and take away barriers to buying)

Product delivery (especially if yours are digital products but also good if you can work with a fulfilment house)

Look at where you are spending your time answering the same questions,

REPURPOSE

Repurposing is just a posh way of saying 'get as many uses out of one thing as you can'. In my case I repurpose my blogs. In other words, my blogs turn into loads of new and different things, based on the same content. One blog can turn into:

- Facebook posts
- Tweets
- Instagram posts
- Pins on Pinterest
- Google+ posts and hangouts
- YouTube videos
- Vimeo videos
- Facebook videos
- LinkedIn posts
- Slideshare slides
- Podcasts
- Guest blogs
- E-books
- Irresistible freebies to help me build my subscriber list
- Content for a book
- Content for teaching classes
- Content for speaking gigs
- Content for webinars
- Memes

I'm sure there are more but that's a good start and a great way to make one piece of content go a long way. How can you use this in your business? Repurposing saves you time and energy. You're not always having to come up with new content and you're not reinventing the wheel each time.

BOUNDARIES

You can't work smarter if you don't have boundaries. Boundaries stop you saying 'yes' to everything. Boundaries let you work on what YOU want to work on and stop you having to react immediately to every question or enquiry. Boundaries mean that you get control of your business and don't let customers, especially needy, bad-fit customers, dictate how you run your business. This is especially important during school holidays but is a big issue all year round. If you put boundaries in place, it will make your life so much easier.

Boundaries can involve the type of people you want to work with, the times you work, the type of work you do, your response times to enquiries, lots of key areas in your business.

The thing is, people can't respect an invisible boundary so you have to set out your boundaries, publicly, and respect them yourself – otherwise they are meaningless.

In term time your boundaries might be:

- I respond to enquiries and emails within 2 working days
- I don't work weekends
- I don't work evenings
- I don't deal with people who don't respect me, or my business
- I work with whom I choose – I reserve the right to say no
- I only do pre-booked work
- I don't give out my home details

During school holidays these might be expanded to include:

- Between June and September our holiday hours are Mon, Wed, Fri from 10-4
- Our response times are up to 3 working days
- We have a Summer waiting list for orders/bookings – please enquire
- The business will be closed between 1st and 14th August

Knowledge is power and if your customers know your boundaries, they can work around them. They will know they can expect to wait longer and if they need you between 1 & 14 August, it aint gonna happen.

This is not unprofessional, despite what helpful friends and family (or your mind monkeys) might tell you. This is the opposite. This is you thinking like a business owner, informing people of where they stand. Much better to do it this way than mislead people into thinking it's business as usual then beat yourself up because you simply don't have time to do the work and will have to let them down. Manage your business like a business, not like a 'little old me hobby'.

FIND TIME WHERE OTHERS WOULDN'T

The thing that sets you apart from other business owners is that now you're in possession of all this new knowledge, from Super Customers to braindumps, 10 minute lists to repurposing, you're a school holiday business ninja. You can find time where others can't.

When others assume school holidays = no work, you have a different mindset. You know you can find time when others would be sitting watching TV, waiting around at dance class or watching kids hurl themselves off play equipment at soft play.

You know you can find time every day, even if only for a few minutes, to keep your business on track and making money. You know how to plan ahead, how to schedule your marketing, how to squeeze every ounce of value out of a piece of content and how to automate whole sections of your business, saving you loads of time and keeping your customers happy.

Your school holiday business ninja tricks know no bounds. Go forth and build your business where others dare not.

MONEY

School holidays can be an expensive time for business owner mums – it's not just the fact that you are often making less money because you're on reduced hours, school holidays COST you, too.

From fuel for 'mum's taxi' to extra pocket money for the children, the magically emptying fridge while the kids are off school, money for days out, activities, holiday clubs – that's not even factoring in any family holidays away from home. It all adds up and the maths doesn't look good. Fewer working hours = less money, kids at home = more money required than usual. Ack! If you haven't planned for this, it can be a bit of a shock when realisation hits.

EASING THE SCHOOL HOLIDAY MONEY SITUATION

There are a few simple things you can do right now, that will help the money situation:

1. Kick start sales
2. Save money where you can
3. Put up your prices
4. Look for additional revenue streams
5. Create more work time
6. Stop kidding yourself

1. KICK START SALES

There's a whole section in this book about kick starting holiday sales, so why not spend a bit of time trying out some of my ideas?

From looking at what you already have in stock, or can easily sell, to quickly creating new, tailored products or services that your customers need right now, there are loads of things you can do to get customers buying.

2. SAVE MONEY WHERE YOU CAN

Have a look in mum's groups in your town. See who's found the deals and money-off vouchers. See what's going on for kids that is free or super-cheap. Loads of businesses and councils will put activities on where the kids can have loads of fun and you can grab a chair, whip out your notebook and create business brilliance. In the Work From Anywhere Girl section you'll find tons of ideas for business 'stuff' you can do if you find yourself out and about, either with or without wifi.

Where I live, and without me even searching, I know that the local council is putting on loads of kids' activities for free in the town centre, each week of the holidays. I also know that our local pet store chain is having lots of free children's workshops and our favourite soft play centre has a packed calendar of activities – we planned ahead and bought an annual pass so all our soft play time is covered - all we pay is a tiny amount to cover materials for some of the cooking/crafty/arty session they put on.

If I REALLY put some effort into searching, I bet I could find something free or super-affordable to do with Chloe every day of the holidays and a lot of those things would let me work at the same time, if I wanted.

3. PUT UP YOUR PRICES

If the thought of putting up your prices makes your bum clench and your heart beat a little too fast, let's talk. Putting up your prices can feel scary when you think about it – what if all my customers leave? What if no-one buys, ever? What if my business folds and I'm destitute?

Did you know, it takes as much effort to sell a £10 product as it does a £100 product – it's all down to your confidence in yourself and your business. Rather than being ruled by fear of 'what if', why not think like a business owner and price your products based on the value you provide to your super customers?

You can put your prices up immediately for new customers and focus on marketing to your Super Customers, so you attract those people who are most likely to buy.

You can gradually introduce a price increase to existing customers, let them know it's coming and make them feel looked after and appreciated. The right ones will stick with you because they see your value.

WHAT HAPPENS WHEN YOU PUT UP YOUR PRICES?

Actually, putting up your prices can work magic in lots of ways that aren't always obvious. When you put up your prices:

- You are making a public statement – one that says 'I'm confident in my products or service and I'm worth this'. It might feel scary but it's great for your self-esteem.

- You have to sell less to make the same money.

- If you sell the same amount you usually do, you'll make MORE money for the same amount of work.

- You put off all those people who were just shopping around on price and weren't loyal

- You attract Super Customers who value you and the service you provide – people who are willing to pay more because your business is a perfect fit for their needs.

4. FIND ADDITIONAL REVENUE STREAMS

How else can you plug the money gap? Can you join an affiliate scheme and sell other people's products to your crowd in return for a share of the profits? Can you sell your products or services online? Can you put together quick training classes or workshops and sell them online? Can you use sell surplus stock on Ebay or Gumtree? Can you try new sales outlets like Etsy or Folksy? Can you offer your services in your spare time via PeoplePerHour or Elance? If you can't plug the money gap with your existing business, be open-minded and think about what you COULD do to bring in some extra money when you need to – not just in the school holidays.

5. CREATE MORE WORK TIME

I've got a whole section on helping you find and create more time for your business during the school holidays, AND on helping you make the most of the extra time you find. A quick way to make more money during the school holidays is to fit in more work – if you want to.

6. STOP KIDDING YOURSELF

Sometimes it feels easier to ignore the fact we're broke and stick a load of stuff on a credit card, but then we have to pay it back and it doesn't feel like such a good idea after all. Don't be tempted to say 'sod it' and spend when you don't have the money – it's far better to spend a little time finding free and low cost things to do that mean you can still spend time with the children AND get some work done.

HOW TO PRICE LIKE A BUSINESS OWNER

If you're not sure that your pricing is right, spend 10 minutes thinking about this. If your pricing is wrong you might be only just covering your costs or at worst, losing money every time you sell something. **If you are not making a profit, you are not running a business. You have an expensive hobby**. Not good. So how SHOULD you price your products or services?

Know Your Costs

How much does it really cost you to provide your service or make & deliver your products? You need to know, it's important.

Direct Costs include:
- **Materials /Ingredients / Components** (even if you already had them in the house)
- **Your Time**
- **Cost of staff or support services to provide that product/service**

Then you have the indirect costs that need to be covered throughout the year by your sales, so it's good to set your prices to include a contribution to these annual costs

- **Premises Rent/Rates**
- **Equipment**
- **Electricity/Water** (if you work from home, take your quarterly bill and allocate a proportion to your business, about 10% is a good start)
- **Marketing & Advertising**
- **Stalls/Stands/Trade shows**

One of my lovely clients makes beautiful handbags. She had a huge stash of material in her house because she collects it. She wasn't selling many bags but she was focusing on selling to shops at a wholesale price, because she thought it would be the easiest way to make money.

When she worked out her costs of components and replacing her fabric stash (not including her time) she got a massive shock. She realised that she was only just covering her material costs at full price. At wholesale price, she was PAYING the shops to take her bags. She was making a big loss. She quickly stopped the wholesale arrangement, put up her prices to reflect the materials AND her time. She started selling on Etsy and finally started MAKING A PROFIT.

Once you know your costs, add in your time and THEN add some on to make a profit. How much profit is up to you and what you think your products/services are worth to your Super Customers.

HOW TO PRICE YOUR TIME

Lots of women find it really difficult to price their time, especially when it's something they enjoy doing and would probably be doing it as a hobby even if it wasn't their business. The trouble is, it's not a hobby. It's a business. And you DO need to price your time.

My advice would be to look at the MINIMUM hourly rate you would work for somebody else for, whether it's £10 or $15 or more and price your time at that rate.

Why would you work for yourself at a lower rate than you'd work for someone else? You're worth it. This is your business, so take control.

If pricing your time at a fair hourly rate makes your products or services feel overly expensive you have 3 choices:

1. Work for pennies just to justify a low price to your customers (no, this is not a good option)
2. Drastically lower your costs – find cheaper materials or take less time
3. Put up your prices and find people who value what you sell – your Super Customers will pay more because you are a perfect fit for them.

GOALS, TARGETS AND FORECASTS

You might think these are only for big businesses, but you'd be wrong. Think about it, if you don't have goals, targets and forecasts, how can you tell how well you're doing? How can you tell whether you're going in the right direction?

How can you tell if you're moving forwards, standing still or going backwards, other than a vague sense of 'having enough money' or 'feeling quite broke' at the end of the month?

During challenging times like the school holidays, it's even more important to understand how much money you have coming in, how much you can expect to come in and how much you are short (so you can do something about it and plug the gap)

So, here are a few questions you need to answer:
1. How much money would you like to take out of the business this year?
2. How much is that per month? (Divide by 12)
3. How many products/services do you need to sell to bring in that amount? And not just sales, it's the amount of PROFIT that matters.

This is where you get your wake up call. Based on your current sales, is that achievable? If not what are you going to do about it? (Read my section on Driving Holiday Sales for a start).

Important: If your target is so high that it's just not possible to achieve, even in your wildest dreams then you have two choices:
1. Revise your expectations and lower your targets accordingly
2. Put up your prices and increase your profits so that you don't have to sell as many things to achieve those targets

What You Need To Do
1. Set your annual and monthly targets and aim to hit them. Make that your main focus. Where you place your attention is where the magic happens.
2. Set up a spreadsheet to track and forecast your sales, month by month (you can download mine here)
3. Update that spreadsheet AT LEAST once a week and if you see you are not on track, do something about it

6 WAYS TO CONJURE UP MONEY QUICKLY

There are other ways to quickly bring money into your business when you need it. Not all of them will be work for you, but some might – and that could make all the difference.

CHASE OUTSTANDING INVOICES NOW!

If you have got people who owe you money...chase them!

It's usually the people who shout the loudest that get paid first – if you are afraid it will jeopardise your relationship with the customer if you chase them, get a virtual assistant or freelance credit controller to make the calls for you.

The fact is, it's money owed to you and it should be in YOUR bank, not subsidising THEIR business. Think like a business owner!

INVOICE AT THE END OF THE JOB, NOT THE END OF THE MONTH

If you've been sitting there with invoices not ready to go out because you only invoice at the end of the month, start invoicing when the job is finished!

Who says that they have to go out at the end of the month? – They don't! If you invoice once the work is done, you'll have a nice steady trickle of cash into the business all the time rather than big chunks that might or might not appear some time 30-90 days after the end of the month you invoice…

REDUCE YOUR CREDIT TIME

Stop giving people 30 days or more to pay. Change your terms and reduce your credit time to 7 days or 14 days. For new customers, ask for an up front payment or at least a hefty deposit to secure their order/spot– this is what a business owner would do. Your business needs regular injections of cash to survive, especially during school holidays when your hours are limited, so make your payment terms suit YOU.

CREATE A SPECIAL CUSTOMER DEAL

Rather than just chasing after new customers all the time, put together some kind of really special deal or offer for your existing customers who love you, know you, have bought from you and recommend you to friends. Give them a deadline to take up the offer. If it's compelling enough, you could bring in a lovely bunch of sales AND make your customers feel loved at the same time.

HOLD A FLASH SALE!

I hold Flash Sales a couple of times a year – everything in my shop is better than half price. I don't give any warning, I just announce them to my crowd and say the deal is on for 48 hours and I sell LOADS. Flash sales are brilliant for driving impulse buyers, impulse sales and also people who just think this is too good to miss. What could you sell? Do you have excess stock you can offer? Do you have end of line stuff you can sell? Do you have self study courses or classes you can reduce down? This is about driving fast sales and making quick money – the products go back up to their usual price after the sale ends.

'DIP YOUR TOE' OFFERS

Can you let people dip their toe in the water so they can try what you offer without a big initial investment or long commitment? Can you promote sample sizes? Taster sessions? How about one month's membership with no on-going commitment? How can you make it easy for them to buy? This way you will get money coming in from the 'tasters' AND you might get some lovely new long-term customers too.

THE SCHOOL HOLIDAY CHILDCARE CHALLENGE

I have 3 sorts of time in the school holidays:

1. Chloe/Family time
2. Work time
3. Combo time

Number one is when we are out together as a family. If my husband is off work, we'll either have time at home together or we'll take trips out as a family. I might grab my 'work from anywhere bag' and stick it in the boot but the idea of these days is that it's a non-work day - it's time spent together, making the most of the holiday. We try to have a good sprinkling of these each school holiday.

Number two is when Chloe is out at dance camp, staying at Grandma's house, or off on a school holiday club trip. I just need to drop her off and she is away for the day, or longer having a wonderful time and I just need to collect her at the end of it. The time in between is mine all mine. That's work time for me. I can go home and crack on.

Number three - Combo time is how I spend most of the school holidays. It's when I have Chloe with me but I still have to work. It involves lots of workarounds and compromises and lots of fun too. Chloe is at the heart of it, we only do stuff she is happy with because let's face it, the reasons I am running my business to be able to give her a good life. We're quite good at finding places where she is happy and I can work, while still giving her the time and attention she needs when she needs it.

COMBO TIME

SOFT PLAY

I cunningly planned ahead and have a VIP membership of my local soft play centre. It is an annual pass that costs me £120 per year and gives Chloe and me unlimited entries, which sounds expensive until you work out what I save, ESPECIALLY during school holidays.

Usual price £7 for Chloe and £1 for me. We can stay all day if we like. There is wifi and a great food/coffee bar.

During the school holidays it becomes a sub-office of The Girls Mean Business, especially in bad weather (it's also great in the sunshine because the outdoor area is one giant sandpit, filled with toys and play equipment).

If I went 15 times in the 8-9 weeks Chloe is off over the summer, I have covered my costs. As it is, I usually spend most Saturday afternoons there having a biz/play date with my business manager Emma and her children, so I have covered my costs during the rest of the year. The school holidays come for free.

OUT AND ABOUT

This applies to anywhere outside really, from the beach to the park, from days out in the forest to long train or plane journeys; the only differentiating factor is whether or not somewhere has wifi.

There are loads of ideas for 'out and about' Combo time working in the Work From Anywhere Girl section.

Combo time when you're out about can be really productive and you ditch that mum guilt. The kids are happy, you get work done if you feel like it = win-win.

WORK FROM ANYWHERE KIT

I have a bag that's always packed and ready, a bit like the bag you take into hospital except this one isn't full of baby stuff, it's full of work stuff. Depending on your business, you might be able to pack all sorts of useful things that mean you can work from anywhere.

In my case, I need a laptop (if there's wifi) or my iPad and phone if there isn't - my tablet has a built in SIM card so I can still get internet access in the remotest of places.

I also take my chargers with me because you never know when you might come across an unexpected plug socket where you can give your laptop/phone a quick top up charge (cafes are pretty obliging about this, in general).

I also need my notebook, a few pens (I love the erasable ones because I can do mind maps and content planning and rub out stuff as I go), my purse, a bottle of water, some baby wipes (just because) and that's about it.

Even if I only have a notebook and pen I can get loads done - I use any spare time to plan out blogs, social media posts or just have a bit of a mini brainstorm with myself.

I can travel pretty light. If I'm taking the car I use my lovely flowery Cath Kidston holdall because I can just sling it in the boot and my work can come with me. If I'm out and about on the train or without the car, I have a small rucksack that everything fits into. Easy peasy.

That bag becomes my work from anywhere kit.

I can work in the car, on a train, on a plane, at the beach, at soft play, in a park, by the river, in the gymnastic club waiting room - pretty much anywhere so if Chloe is happy, occupied, fed and watered then I can use that time (if I want) to work.

I don't, always.

Sometimes I have a great time chatting to Chloe or watching Chloe. Sometimes my head isn't in the right place for work so I just people-watch and have a rest but lots of the time I get work done. In the Work From Anywhere Girl chapter I'll share a load of little jobs that I get done when I'm out and about in Combo time that might help you too.

TIPS FOR CRAFTERS AND MAKERS

If you're a crafter or a maker, think about taking piecework out and about with you. What can you prep? What can you cut out? Pin? Sketch? What parts of your regular work and preparation can be done outside when you have an hour or two here and there?

Use your imagination and see if you can get ahead of yourself - any prep you can do during Combo time is a job you don't have to do when you've got dedicated work time.

PLAN CHILDCARE IN ADVANCE

Let's be honest, it really helps if you can plan your childcare even a little ahead. It doesn't have to be months in advance but do start thinking about how you'll manage the holiday, even if it's a week or two away.

Apart from getting brownie points for being super-organised, there are other benefits to planning ahead. The first is that it will save you time and money.

THE EARLY BIRD GETS THE WORM

I could have saved £10 on an early bird booking for a drama workshop Chloe wanted to attend in the school holidays, if I'd booked before the deadline. I didn't put it in my calendar, so I forgot! Gah!

Loads of clubs and events use the early bird discount model. They do it because it helps them to gauge interest early on - if no-one takes them up on it then they'll probably cancel but if their early bird offer does well then they know they'll probably fill the places.

Also it helps with their cash-flow because they have money to cover the set up and marketing.

Your job is to look out for kids' activities with early bird booking deadlines, well in advance.

REPENT AT LEISURE

Many holiday clubs and activities get booked up quickly, which is another reason to plan well ahead.

Don't be left fuming in the first week of the holidays because everything good is already fully booked, just because you didn't think to plan ahead.

IT'S NEVER TOO LATE TO PLAN

If you're reading this part way through the school holidays (and wishing you'd found it sooner) don't worry! It's never too late to plan. Even if you just start planning a day or two ahead, you can get some structure to your week and stop fire-fighting.

Ask around in online mums groups in your area. See what's going on.

If you're too late to book any activities, see if you can organise a play date for the kids.

BIZ/PLAY DATES

If you have friends who are also business owner mums then do what I do with Emma, my business manager and organise Biz/Play dates.

We meet at soft play or the park, at a garden centre or one of our houses and the kids play together while we chat and work.

It means we get loads done and have a good old catch up while still being there for the children.

CHILDCARE SWAPS

If you don't have business mum friends, ask one of the other school mums if she'd like to do a bit of childcare swapping. School holidays can be a tiring time so I'm sure you'll find willing volunteers to take your children for a day if you return the favour and take theirs on another day.

SHOULD I SHUT THE SHOP?

If your business runs from premises, especially if you're in retail then everyone will expect your shop to be open as usual.

After all you are still paying rent, rates, utilities so it's even more expensive if you have to shut it because you don't have any income to contribute to those costs. This presents probably the trickiest situation over the school holidays - lots of us can simply work from home or book fewer slots but you retail girls have it tricky.

So what can you do over the school holidays?

Well, if your kids are older then it's not so much of an issue - they can either spend time with friends, go off and do their own thing or help you in the shop. If you've got younger children then you're going to have to be resourceful unless you want bored, fractious little ones stuck in the shop with you all day.

YOUR OPTIONS

I asked retail business owners on my Facebook page 'The Girls Mean Business' how they cope in the school holidays, to see whether they have any little nuggets of information or any tips or hints that will help you.

Actually, what came out was that most people just muddle through – There is no secret recipe to make this work, you just have to use workarounds.

GET HELP

One big piece of advice that came across was that you need to get help. Help with the children, and help to run the shop.

HELP (WO)MANNING THE SHOP

The good thing about school holidays is that there are lots of students around, and although it may seem like a hassle to interview and reference check a whole bunch of students, you might hit it lucky and find somebody you can help you every school holidays, at least for a couple of years while they are studying.

Better still, see if any of your friends or acquaintances have children who are trustworthy and looking for extra income - Let's face it students are always broke.

At least if you have a connection, if anything does go wrong then you have parents to hold accountable.

Yes, you will have to pay them, but that just means that you have to start thinking like a business owner. A business owner should have enough working capital in the business to be able to afford staff because, let's face it, you have other jobs to do apart from standing behind a counter. You may love working in the shop, but other people can do that job just as well are you need to make time to spend on the business, not just IN the business.

You need to be making a good profit, enough to pay your salary and pay for help when you need it as well as other business expenses like rent, rates, marketing, etc. If you are finding it hard to make a profit and then you need to look at your business objectively before it's too late.

WHAT IS GOING WRONG?

Are you not getting the footfall? Are people coming into the shop but not buying? Are you not taking advantage of social media to drive traffic and sales?

Whether or not you have the right premises for your business is a whole different topic - suffice to say that if you are very clear on your Super Customers and you are marketing to attract them and either they are not coming, or they are coming and not buying, then there is a mismatch somewhere that you need to address.

HELP WITH THE CHILDREN

Do you have trusted friends or family who could help you for a couple of days over the school holidays?

My advice would be not to push your luck and ask people for lots of help because you will overwhelm them and stop them ever offering again. Instead, ask people if they can have your children for maybe one or two days across the holidays and see how it goes. It may be that the aunties, grandparents and friends have a brilliant time and offer to do more - at least that's their choice and they can offer rather than have it foisted upon them by you.

Could you employ a child-minder or a nanny for a couple of days a week? Again you are going to have to make the money to cover this but that is part of thinking like a business owner. This is where your planning comes in and if you plan ahead, you can factor those expenses into your cash flow and make sure you have time to interview and engage the right people to help you.

Can you make use of holiday schemes at your local soft play area, leisure centre, nursery? Time to get real and start being resourceful – a little bit of planning might give you a pretty structured holiday period with happy children and a relatively unstressed mother.

INVOLVE THE CHILDREN

If you have run out of options or you just want to keep your children with you, which is also fine, then let's look at how you might involve them in the business.

Clearly this is totally dependent on their age, but most kids love helping mummy and playing at being grown up.

My daughter is seven and she is at the stage where housework seems like great fun so I'm making the most of that one!

What could your children do in the shop? If they are slightly older, but still too young to be left alone, could you ask them to do the stock checks or inventory for you?

- Could you get them to set up your social media accounts?
- Could you set them to work on Canva designing
  - posters,
  - flyers,
  - Social media images,
  - vouchers,
  - or anything else that you could genuinely use in the business?

- Could you set them to work setting up spreadsheets or Word templates for you? (Let's face it, Setting up the templates is often the most tricky part, so if they are a whiz on the computer, let's make the most of their skills!)
- Ask them to set up
  - invoice templates,
  - purchase orders,
  - email templates,
  - email signatures with your contact details and social media details on them,
  - spreadsheets,
  - inventory spreadsheets,
  - marketing planning spreadsheets,
  - any spreadsheet that will save you time and effort later on and will encourage you to think like a business owner and track your business numbers.

Here's an idea: why not get them to set up a sales forecast spreadsheet for you with goals and targets for each year and each month, so all you have to do is plug in the figures every week and every month?

If your children are younger, they can still have fun. When I asked about this on Facebook some ladies said that they made their children assistant managers, gave them a little badge, and gave then specific tasks like cleaning or sorting stock, dusting shelves or turning things so that the labels are all pointing in the right direction.

My daughter loves playing on Canva and even though I might not use everything that she makes, she has spent hours happily creating posters and lovely images for free and all I have to do is keep an eye on her and tell her how brilliant she is whenever she shows me anything. I have told her that she is my chief designer at the company business and she is as happy as a clam, especially when I share her art work on Facebook.

Can you make a crafty area for your children, give them each a notebook and scrapbook some glue some glitter some ribbons and paper and stickers and see what they come up with?

HOLIDAY HOURS

Remember as well that you do not have to open from nine till five or your usual hours. You are allowed time off, and you are allowed to work reduced hours.

This is your judgement call. You will know what will work and what won't work, but maybe with a combination of help with manning the shop, help with childcare, and reduced hours you might find that you are able to find a happy balance which gives you some time off with the children, doesn't lead to you shutting the shop too often and losing money, and also keeps your customers happy.

Remember that you can always do far more online over the summer as well so even if you do have to do reduced shop hours, that doesn't mean that your sales need to be down. If you put the effort into your website shop and your social media promotion, you could actually drive a lot of sales even when the shop is shut. And another job for the children could be to help you fulfil online orders. Just a thought!

MARKETING MAGIC FOR THE SCHOOL HOLIDAYS

You are a micro-business owner and a mum. And it's the school holidays. Even working during term time you have got a limited time, money and energy to spend on marketing. During school holidays, you can reduce that to a third or half, so you need to get really smart with your time. And why waste your time trying to attract people who are never going to buy? You may as well market to the people who are really good fit and who are most likely to buy from you. Especially in the school holidays

This is why you need to know your Super Customer - remember I talked about this at the beginning of the book?

Super Customer marketing is clever marketing - it concentrates your limited time, money and energy only on the people who are most likely to buy from you. You are not wasting time, money and energy on people who are not likely to buy.

DON'T DO ANYTHING DRASTIC!

This does not mean that you have to sack any customers or clients. This does not mean that you turn business away. This is not about whom you work with– you can work with and sell to whomever you like, that is your prerogative. This is only about being clever with your marketing.

SUPER CUSTOMER MARKETING

1. Get really clear on who is a great fit for your business, on what type of person is MOST LIKELY to buy from you

2. Figure out WHY they are a great fit? Why do they value you, love what you do, keep coming back? What problems do you solve? What outcome do you bring about?

3. Come up with targeted marketing messaged aimed at your Super Customers, that show them why your business is just what they need (based on your knowledge of them)

4. Work out WHERE they hang out and spend their time, online and offline

5. Put your targeted messages in front of your Super Customers where they hang out

6. Repeat (5) little and often

The idea of Super Customer marketing is to get them virtually nodding their heads when they read your marketing – you need to create OMG moments. An OMG moment is when somebody sees your marketing and recognises themselves so clearly in what you've written that they have an moment when they say "OMG that is me! She is talking about me! She is a mind reader! I need her!" It is called self-selection and you can definitely do it with your marketing if you know your Super Customers.

OK, let's get stuck in. Let's talk about blogging, e-newsletters, social media and more. Let's get your marketing rocking over the school holidays!

WHAT DO I WRITE ABOUT?

It's all very well knowing you need to keep marketing but what do you write about in your blogs, e-newsletters and social media posts?

Try my Clever Content Generator system

1. Find 3 topics you can talk about easily, that your Super Customers will love
2. Break each of the 3 down into smaller sub-topics
3. Break the sub-topics down further
4. Result = tons of content ideas!

In my business my 3 topics could be marketing, productivity and confidence. If I take MARKETING, I can break it down into lots of sub-topics, which can be further broken down. I can do the same for each of my big topics. I'll NEVER run out of content ideas.

CLEVER CONTENT GENERATOR SYSTEM

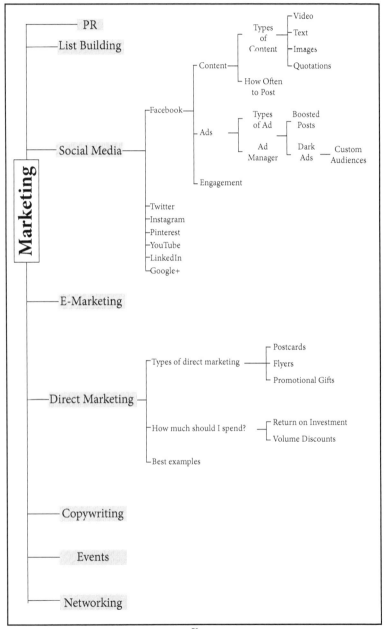

YOUR BIG TOPICS

- How might this work for you?
- What can you easily write about?
- What would your Super Customers find interesting?
- What could your 3 big topics be?
- If you can think of more, then great! The more the better.

EXAMPLES

Massage Therapist
1. Types of massage
2. What conditions massage can help
3. How massage works

Toy Shop Owner
1. Best toys for different ages
2. Toys & Learning
3. New Toy Ranges

Crochet Baby Clothes Business
1. Styles of crochet baby clothes
2. Upcycling crochet baby clothes
3. Handmade Heirlooms

Accountant
1. Tax for scaredy cats
2. Book-keeping made easy
3. Hints and tips to save you money

Artist
1. Examples of your work
2. Ideas and Inspiration
3. Work in progress – behind the scenes

Weight Loss Business
1. Why we get fat
2. Biggest myths about weight loss
3. Safe, easy & manageable ways to lose weight

Do you get the idea? This will be easier for some businesses than others. With things like crafts – handbags, baby clothes, soaps – you need to think about WHY people are buying.

WHY DO THEY BUY?

- If they buy a bag, do they want to look good? Buy something unique? Support handmade businesses? If you know your Super Customer, you'll be able to see what makes them buy from you and you can work out what they would be interested in.
- If they buy handmade soap is it because they want their house to smell beautiful? To impress guests? To go chemical-free? Again, if you know why they buy, you can write about things you know they will find interesting.
- If they buy handmade crocheted baby clothes is it because they want unique pieces they can keep and hand down? Is it because they LOVE crochet? Is it because they LOVE handmade?

Get to the root of why they buy and writing content will become miles easier.

VIDEO

Videos are a GREAT marketing tool because:

- They show you're a real, live person
- They help to build relationships
- They showcase your expertise
- They give you credibility
- They allow you to demonstrate techniques
- They get great reach on Social Media
- They can be used for loads of other things

If you're not doing video marketing, you need to start now. However scared you are (I know!) and however crazy the mind monkeys are going, if you're not doing videos you are missing out.

During school holidays, videos can provide really good content you can use in loads of different ways to help:

- Drive traffic to your website
- Boost your Facebook reach and engagement
- Build your email subscriber list
- SELL more!

VIDEO IDEAS

First of all, don't get hung up on giving away your knowledge. The best businesses are happy to share lots of information because it helps their customers and potential customers to trust them, get to know them and see the quality of what they sell.

1. Demonstrate a technique – even if people can't or don't want to make/do it themselves, it's always interesting to see how things are done.

2. Ask a customer to record you a testimonial

3. Talk through a 'before and after' case study

4. Introduce a product/service range and explain how it works or who it's for

5. Tackle frequently asked questions, one video at a time

6. Share shortcuts and trade secrets you know your Super Customers will love

7. Record video blogs (Vlogs)

8. Interview a supplier

9. Interview a customer

10. Interview an industry expert or author

11. Show how to use a piece of software – you can record your screen for free with www.screencast-o-matic.com

12. Do a time lapse video of a project from start to finish

13. Teach what your Super Customers want to know

14. Create a little video teaching series you can use as an irresistible freebie to get people onto your email list

15. Show us around where you work

16. Show us how you store your equipment

17. Show us your stock collection

18. Show us how you choose what to use for each project

19. Show us the difference between different bits of equipment for the same job

20. Do a product review

21. Do a book review

22. Show us some shortcuts we might not know

VIDEO TIPS

1. Don't get too hung up on the quality. Do the best you can with what you have, whether it's a phone or tablet camera, a webcam or a video camera.

2. Try to get quiet surroundings so your voice can be heard

3. Have the light in front of you, or to the side NOT behind you or you'll show up as a silhouette

4. Try to record out of the wind if you're outside or the wind noise will drown out your voice

5. Have the camera level with your head or pointing just slightly above your eyeline – don't look down at it or it will give you double chins even if you don't have them

6. Smile from the moment you switch on the camera, even if you don't start talking for a few seconds – you won't need to trim off a frowning, puzzled face then

7. Have post it notes with your key talking points stuck to your computer screen if you're using a webcam, so you don't forget or lose your train of thought

8. Look directly at the camera

9. If you're recording with a phone or tablet, a tripod (even a mini tripod) will keep it from shaking.

10. Selfie sticks are great for shooting videos out and about – people don't mind a bit of wobble

11. Have a crib sheet if you're recording your video out and about – you can always pin it to a tree or hold it behind the camera with your other hand if you need reminding what to say

12. Get recording. Your first ones will be awful, just delete them. The more you record, the easier and better it gets

13. Don't fret about having bad hair / a weird voice/ being overweight – I'm all of those things and it hasn't stopped me- people just want to learn

14. Talk to your Super Customer, they will love hearing from you. Don't worry about what anyone else thinks

15. Be you! People want to learn from you – you are perfect as you are

16. You are an expert – talk with passion about what you know. You know more than you think and you know more than most other people about your topic

17. If your video sound is rubbish, invest in a microphone. The one I started with is the Samson GoMic

18. Always be looking for opportunities to create videos – out and about with the kids is a brilliant time to record short snippets and tips to upload to Facebook or YouTube

19. Keep them short – you can always do longer ones later as you get more confidence. 30 seconds is fine if you've said what you need to say

20. B.R.E.A.T.H.E

21. S.L.O.W D.O.W.N

22. Enjoy it, have a laugh, be yourself – your Super Customers will love you

23. People love REAL – share some behind the scenes footage and give them a glimpse into your business and life

BLOGS

I love blogs. They are a fantastic way to show what you do, share what you know, build relationships with customers and potential customers and drive traffic to your website.

If you don't already have a blog, Wordpress is an easy place to start. I've got some 'getting started with Wordpress Blogs' videos in the Book Bonus section – Emma, my business manager recorded these for you to get you started.

What can you write about?

Look at **Try my Clever Content Generator system in the What Can I Write About section** and you should get loads of ideas.

WHY BLOGS ARE BRILLIANT

Blogs are the whole foundation of my business. One blog can turn into LOADS of different things including:

- Podcasts

- Videos

- Facebook Posts

- Tweets

- Pins

- Posts on Instagram

- LinkedIn Posts

- Slideshare Presentations

- E-Newsletter content

And that's just a few.

Blogs also help you get found in Google searches because with each blog you're creating new content for your website. Google LOVES fresh new content, especially if you create it regularly so a good new blog every month is perfect.

With each blog you'll be covering different topics your Super Customers will love, and will be searching for on Google, so you're increasing the ways you can be found.

Blogs are great for

- Teaching

- Sharing your knowledge

- Showing you know your stuff

- Building your online profile

- Building relationships with fans

- Showing how you think

- NOT reinventing the wheel every time you need content

People buy people and blogs are a great way for people to get to know you and see that you are an expert.

Blogs are easy to write. A 500 word blog is about the right length to get you found in the search results and you can be strategic with your blogging too.

What are your Super Customers searching for on Google?

Mine are searching for:

- Get more customers
- Attracting new customers
- How to sell more
- Get more confidence
- Get more done
- Running a business with children
- Help with pricing / How to price my products / services
- Easy marketing tips
- Free marketing ideas
- Cheap marketing ideas
- How to run business in school holidays

Because I know what they are searching for, I can write blogs that will help answer those questions. And when they put in those searches to Google, there's a good chance my blogs will appear.

WHAT ARE YOURS SEARCHING FOR?

Spend 10-15 minutes brainstorming – get inside the head of your Super Customers and figure out what they will be putting into Google, that you can help them with. Look at all the different aspects – think about your 3 big topics we talked about earlier and how your Super Customer might phrase or word their Google searches.

The beauty of blogs is that you can write them in advance and have them scheduled to go out during the school holidays. You can automate them so they publish on a certain date, so your website is updated when you're out at the beach or at soft play.

1. Write for your Super Customer – don't try to please everyone

2. Make your blog title fit with something your Super Customers are searching for – 'How To Upcycle Baby Clothes' rather than 'Look What I Made', for example.

3. Break your blog down into smaller sections with headings, it makes it easier to scan and read

4. Make sure your sub-headings also help you get found – 'Upcycling Jeans Into Baby Bibs' rather than 'How Cute Is This?'. You still say 'how cute is this' but have it in the blog copy rather than the headings.

5. Break your blog up with images that either illustrate what you're describing (your own photos are great) or appropriate stock images – and make sure you add an image description behind the scenes when you upload the image – that will help you get found too. Again, think strategically when you describe your images – what is your Super Customer searching for?

6. Be yourself – you're trying to attract people who love you as you are

7. If you have a Wordpress site, install YOAST – a free SEO (Search Engine Optimisation) plug-in to help you get found

8. Write about things you love and that interest you – it will come easier

9. Have a list building sign-up box at the end of each blog (I use the Magic Action Box plug-in for Wordpress but there are other options)

10. Share your blog EVERYWHERE! Don't rely on people finding it on their own, share it all over social media every few weeks

E-NEWSLETTERS

E-newsletters are one of my FAVOURITE school holiday marketing tools and they are seriously under-rated.

You can write and schedule them before the holidays so they go out every couple of weeks, keeping you top of mind and even driving sales while you're out and about with the family.

If you've not done e-newsletters before, start as soon as you can! There are 2 things you need to have in place to get started:

1. Email Marketing software
2. People to send the newsletter to

After that it's all about the content.

EMAIL MARKETING SOFTWARE

You MUST use proper email marketing software for 2 reasons.

1 Firstly, you need to conform to the spam laws and proper e-marketing software handles all this for you, letting people easily unsubscribe and telling them how they got onto your list. If you don't use proper software and use your own email address instead, if someone puts in a spam complaint about you (it happens more often than you might think) then ALL your emails will be blacklisted and your account might even get shut down. Eek!

2 The second reason to use proper email marketing software is because of the brilliant marketing information you get – it will tell you how many people opened your newsletters and when, which links were clicked and by whom and how many people unsubscribed.

This is invaluable because you can see if your newsletters are hitting the mark – if lots of people are clicking through to your site but not buying, either you are attracting the wrong people onto your email list or they are not getting what they expect when they reach your site. If hardly anyone is opening it, is it because your newsletter titles are boring? Or spammy so they go straight into the spam bin? If you know what's happening when your e-newsletters go out, you can do something with that information not just during school holidays, but all the time.

Most email marketing packages work in the same way, so if you don't want to use Mailchimp you can still follow the steps in your preferred system.

The one I usually recommend is Mailchimp because it has a GREAT starter package with enough free emails for most small businesses. It has a really useful help section too. If you want to get started with Mailchimp we've got some FAB FREE 'how to' videos to walk you through setting up and sending an e-newsletter –
get them here: www.bitly.com/sosbizbook

7 THINGS YOU NEED TO DO TO GET UP AND RUNNING WITH AN E- NEWSLETTER

1. Choose your email marketing software & set up an account

2. Set up a LIST (call it 'newsletter' or 'web signups')

3. Create a sign up form (or opt-in form) and either paste the code into your website* or create a sign-up tab on Facebook **

4. Set up a TEMPLATE to make your newsletter look lovely

5. Write your newsletter

6. Press send

7. See how the stats look after 24 hours

If this sounds scary, why not pay for an hour or two of a virtual assistant's time and get them to do it for you? It will be simple for them and most of it is a one-off job – once it's set up you can overwrite it for each new newsletter.

*if the thought of code brings you out in hives, again ask a virtual assistant to set up the sign-up form in your website or ask your web person to do it for you

**Mailchimp has an 'integrations' section to help you link your Facebook page and create a tab but be aware tabs don't currently show up on mobile devices

CAN I ADD CUSTOMERS TO MY SUBSCRIBER LIST?

The simple answer is yes, if they are recent (usually if they have purchased within the last year). When you set up a list in your e-newsletter software it will ask you to write a short statement telling your subscribers how they got onto your list.

Mine goes something like this:

'You are receiving this newsletter because you've bought something from me (thank you!), you've downloaded one of my free business resources or you've signed up for one of my webinar classes. You can easily unsubscribe by clicking the link at the bottom of this email'

DO NOT!

Add people into your list who have not bought from you and who have not given you permission. This means don't add:

- People who have given you their business card at some point
- People who are on a list you've bought
- People who are on a list you've found on the internet
- People who were supposed to be blind-copied in an email you received, but weren't

Apart from breaking a ton of spam laws you are not helping your business in any way. If someone hasn't knowingly and willingly signed up to your list, you are going to get loads of spam complaints and people are not going to be engaged and buy.

You want people on your subscriber list who WANT to be there. Who have signed up because they love what you do. They want to receive your emails – yay! You need to be transparent and open about the fact people are going to be added to your mailing list / subscriber list so when you embed your sign up form in your site make sure you say 'you'll also receive my regular newsletter and occasional promotional emails' or whatever you're comfortable with, so people know to expect it.

WHAT DO I PUT IN MY E-NEWSLETTER?

Well, if you're not sure what topics to write about, use my **Clever Content Generator system** on page 78.

Then, think about which e-newsletters YOU enjoy reading. What do you like to see? Personally, I love a little personal introduction, a useful article, maybe some tips and resources, anything that will help me build my business.

What would YOUR Super Customers love? What do they want? What do they need? What can you share?

Here are some ideas:

- Personal introduction
- Tips & hints
- Short cuts
- Trade secrets
- Books you would recommend
- Great websites you love and use
- Book reviews
- Equipment reviews
- A video about a product or service
- Inspiration quotes
- A product showcase
- An offer or deal (these need to be used sparingly or your subscribers will get sick of being sold to and will unsubscribe)

SCHOOL HOLIDAY LIST-BUILDING MACHINE

The great thing about growing your email list is you can set it up to work 24 hours a day, without you thinking about it.

Building your email list or subscriber list is super-important because Social Media is fickle and you can't rely on that alone to market your business. The rules change, your account could go wonky, anything could happen and you have no control – your business would be at the mercy of Facebook or Twitter and that's not a good position to be in.

Take back control of your marketing and build an email list of your Super Customers so you can market to them when YOU want, not when your chosen Social Media platform decides to show it to them.

The good news is, you can create an irresistible freebie or two (I'll tell you how that works in a mo) and set up a little list building machine while out and about during the school holidays. Using scheduled Social Media posts and maybe a few ads, you can create a little list building machine that runs itself in the background, no matter what you're doing.

HOW I USE MY EMAIL LIST

I've spent 3 years building my email list and I have over 20,000 amazing women business owners signed up. They get a weekly e-newsletter from me packed with useful, valuable information and I get great feedback about it.

Then, when I have something they can buy, I send out an email to my subscribers with a special offer and wow, does that work! People buy, because I'm not selling to them all the time, so when I DO have something they will like, they are very receptive.

I have sold £18,000 worth of products before from ONE email.

That's because I've looked after my subscribers, given them great free content they can use to build their business and don't constantly spam them or sell to them. I really value my list. It's the most valuable part of my business and it should be for you, too.

HORROR STORY:

A few years ago I had a panic email from a lady who sells handbags. She has no website because she buys end of line handbags from a warehouse and as soon as she advertises them on her Facebook page, they sell like hot cakes. She's never needed a site.

She had been running 'like and share' competitions on her Facebook page, which are against Facebook's promotional guidelines. Facebook had warned her against it a couple of times but she took no notice.

One day she woke up and her page with 4000 fans was gone. GONE!

She had no email list. The only contact details she had were from people who had bought via Paypal. She had to start again. From scratch. Overnight her business was GONE.

She emailed me in a panic and I shared her new page on my page to help her get started again but I told her to start building her email list right away – to offer a discount coupon or run LEGAL competitions on Facebook where people give their email address and go into a prize draw, so she would never be in that position again. True story.

Don't let that happen to you – BUILD YOUR LIST!

HOW DO I GET PEOPLE ONTO MY SUBSCRIBER LIST?

The simple answer is, you encourage and tempt them to sign up with an irresistible freebie. Your irresistible freebie needs to be a FILTER and a MAGNET.

1. It needs to filter out people who are not a good fit for your business
2. It needs to be a magnet to attract your Super Customers because they are most likely to buy

My irresistible freebie is '55 Fabulous 10-Minute Marketing Tips For Women Business Owners' and it works brilliantly because it's aimed at my Super Customers. They are women who are struggling with marketing and short on time, so my free e-book is just what they need.

WHAT COULD YOUR IRRESISTIBLE FREEBIE BE?

What would tempt your Super Customers onto your list?

What could you give them that they would LOVE to get their hands on but that would only attract them if they are a good fit for you?

Here are some ideas for you:

- A free e-book that will save them time and money

- A cheat sheet with 'done for you' examples

- A tick/check list to help them work through something

- A top resources list

- Your 'little black book' of favourite tools/equipment

- A video demonstrating a technique people struggle with

- A screen-share video showing how to use a type of software

- A money off coupon

- A 'trade secrets' sheet

- A 'behind the scenes' video

- A 'top ideas or suggestions' sheet (for gift businesses)

- A top trends this season video/ guide sheet

HOW DO I GET MY FREEBIE TO MY NEW SUBSCRIBERS?

The simplest way to deliver your freebie, especially if you're using Mailchimp is to customise the welcome message when you set up your list. It will give you a standard welcome message but you can be clever and tailor it to say?

"Hello! Thank you for signing up for my free [name of your freebie] – here's a link where you can download it. You will also receive my regular e-newsletter packed with great information and deals. You can unsubscribe at any time"

If it's a video you can host it for free on YouTube and just link to your YouTube video in the welcome message.

If it's a PDF document then you can embed it in your Mailchimp welcome message – it will let you add a document. Easy peasy.

TOP TIP

On Facebook, tabs don't show up on mobile devices. To get around this, create a special 'sign up' page on your website where you put a sign up form and tell people what they are getting – ideally get someone on <u>www. fiverr.com</u> to create an image for you to represent your freebie. My 55 Tips e-book image is set up to look like a real book. My sign up page is <u>www. bitly.com/55tips</u> and I share this everywhere my Super Customers hang out.

HOW DO I GET MORE PEOPLE ONTO MY EMAIL LIST?

Remember you don't want anyone or everyone – you really only want Super Customers on your list.

1. Promote your irresistible freebie everywhere your Super Customers hang out on Social Media

2. Use FB ads to get your irresistible freebie in front of new people

3. Put a short sentence and link to your freebie on the bottom of Facebook posts

4. Tweet about it – include a short description and a link to the sign up page

5. Post your freebie image on Pinterest and Instagram

6. Create a short link on www.bitly.com like mine (www.bitly.com/55tips) and put that link on your business cards and flyers

7. Create a video talking about your fab freebie and share it on social media

8. Use Google Ads to promote your freebie

9. Ask other people with similar audiences to share your freebie if you do the same for them

10. Sponsor a newsletter if you can find one going out to the right people for you – ask if you can include the freebie in your little sponsor section

11. If you put ads in magazines or newspapers, include your short Bitly link to your freebie

12. Put a link to your freebie on the bottom of your blogs

13. Put a link to your freebie on the bottom of any guest blogs you write

14. Shout about your freebie, regularly! Once is not enough!

PR

PR is basically free coverage in the press. It's different to advertising or advertorials that you pay for. PR is when a magazine, website, newpaper, radio or TV station picks up on a story about your business and prints it for free because they know their readers/viewers will find it interesting.

HOW DO YOU GET FREE COVERAGE?

First of all, not all coverage is useful for you. You really want coverage in places your Super Customer hangs out – you want to be featured in newspapers, magazines and on websites they read, radio stations they listen to and TV programmes they watch, otherwise it's wasted.

Getting Started:
1. Get inside the head of your Super Customers
2. Work out what they watch/browse/listen to/read
3. Create a top 10 shortlist of your best newspapers, websites, magazines and TV/radio stations
4. Do your research – get to know your shortlist (more about this in a bit)
5. Get to know the journalists and help them where you can
6. Ask them how to get featured

The reason this works is because every media channel is staffed by real people (gasp!), and they are the people who create the content.

If you can get to know them and help them out, they are going to be much more receptive when you ask them the best way to get featured.

TWITTER IS BRILLIANT FOR THIS!

Twitter is a really good PR tool because if you look in every magazine and watch every news programme, you'll see every reporter and journalist these days has a Twitter handle like this @thegirlsmeanbiz.

Journalists love Twitter because it's like having an ear to the ground – it gives them instant feedback and they can see what's being talked about, so they can jump on it. Also if they need opinions for stories, they can just ask on Twitter and get loads of responses, instantly.

Often journalists will do shoutouts about something specific they are looking for, from 'mums of triplets' to 'businesses using crowdfunding' – they know they will get connections quickly on Twitter.

Your job is to find the journalists who work for your top 10 media shortlist and see which ones cover your sort of business – maybe it's news reporters, features editors, women's editors, you won't know until you do the research. Follow them on Twitter and see what they tweet about, and see where you can help.

Remember they are busy, especially on deadline. Don't stalk or hassle them or they'll soon hit the block button. You need to watch, wait, help, retweet their requests, give your opinions and get to know them a little. Then, ask them for pointers rather than being 'in your face' and harassing the to feature you – after all, you wouldn't like that done to you and you wouldn't do it in person, so don't do it online!

DO YOU NEED A PRESS RELEASE?

Now, I'm sure there are lots of different approaches to the media but this one works well for micro businesses like ours. You might think you need to send out a press release and there's no harm in that BUT don't send it to everyone, everywhere.

Even if you are sending out press releases, it's much better to tailor them to the publication in question and make it fits their profile.

PLANNING & AUTOMATING

Planning your marketing during school holidays means you can pretty much set and forget it, leaving you free to get on and do other things. There is one little tool that makes scheduling easy:

Hootsuite is an easy-to-use little tool you can use on your computer, phone or tablet. The free account is perfect for most micro-business owners because it lets you manage up to 3 social profiles, which is enough for most people. If you need more, the Pro version is only a few pounds per month. It lets you post, schedule, comment and share on most of the Social Media platforms. www.hootsuite.com

Facebook has its own free, built-in scheduler – whenever you create a post on Facebook you have the option to post it now or schedule it to post at some point in the future. You can do this as many times as you like and you can schedule years ahead if you wanted. It's up to you to come up with the posts, schedule them in and go off and enjoy your holiday.

WHAT ELSE CAN YOU SCHEDULE?

Blogs

You can schedule more than just Social Media posts – you can also schedule your blogs to publish at a time of your choosing, so you can write a bunch of blogs and schedule them to go out one per week, or once a month. When you're in a writing mood (and I'm not always, so I make the most of it when I am) then use **Clever Content Generator system** I showed you earlier on page 78 and get writing. You'll be happy you did, when you can set them to schedule and then get on with your school holiday.

E-newsletters

You can write your e-newsletters in advance and schedule them to go out when you like. This means you can take advantage of those times when you're finding writing super easy (as opposed to the times when you can't write for toffee) and write a stack of e-newsletters in one go, then schedule them to go out once a month while you do what you like.

I'd recommend you double check them before they are due to go out just in case there's anything you'd like to add, but otherwise just set and forget. If you're not sure what to talk about in your e-newsletters, check back to the e-newsletters section in this chapter and you'll get some great ideas – also my Clever Content Generator system will mean you won't be stuck for what topics to cover.

Promotional emails

If you have product launches or promotions going on during the school holidays you can write the emails in advance and schedule them with your email marketing software.

WHAT CAN YOU AUTOMATE?

What do you keep repeating in your business? What questions do you seem to answer several times a week? What emails do you always seem to have to write? What do you keep having to do manually, that software could do for you?

Frequently Asked Questions

If there are questions that customers and potential buyers always ask before they buy, write them down and write down your standard answers because you can take the repetition out of this.

Once you have a list of all the questions people ask you about your products, services or business, put them on a page on your website called Frequently Asked Questions. That way potential buyers can get the answers they need without waiting for you to be back online, so it's GREAT customer service and means you don't waste time answering the same questions all the time.

Auto Responders

Now, take your FAQ list and post it into an email auto responder – these are easy to do on most email marketing programmes but I think you need the paid version of Mailchimp – it's still really cost effective.

If people always email 'support@' or 'admin@' then put your FAQ auto responder onto those email accounts. You can put a little prefix on the email that says:

'Hello! If you have a question about our products or services, there's a good chance we have already answered the question here, so check out our frequently asked questions. If you still have questions that aren't answered here, we'll get back to you within 2 working days.'

That way you are managing their expectations and telling people when they can expect to hear from you, which is also GREAT customer service. Yay!

YOUR JOB

Look at everything you do in your business and see what you can do in advance, what you can schedule, what you can automate – see what you can save time now and during the school holidays and you'll be so glad you did!

DRIVING HOLIDAY SALES

If you're determined to make the school holidays count and dispel the myth that it's a 'quiet time' for sales, let's look at how you can proactively get people buying. Only do this if you have a way to fulfil the orders – there's no point driving sales if you're going to let customers down because you don't have time to create the products or deliver the services. That being said, you can always have an offer and campaign aimed at filling up your order book once the schools are back – a pre-booking early bird price.

WHAT CAN YOU SELL RIGHT NOW?

Well? What's sitting there ready to go?

What training programmes or classes do you have already written and set up?

What do you already have in stock?

What services could you easily offer during the school holidays and even outsource to a trusted sub-contractor?

What could you create really quickly and easily that you know would sell?

Time to sit down with a piece of paper and a pen and start brainstorming because I'm sure there is something that you already have or you can easily create that you know you could sell.

I MADE 3K IN 2 WEEKS FOR A HOLIDAY

In 2012 I really needed a winter holiday. My marketing agency had gone into liquidation, I'd just had to pay the liquidators £20k, The Girls Mean Business was doing OK but I didn't have spare cash to take us away for some winter sun.

I needed 3k.

I realised if I could create a really accessible, lovely, attractive short coaching programme and sell it for £99, I only needed to sell 30 to make my 3K. So I scoped it out based on what I was seeing and hearing from my ladies on my Facebook page.

I created a beginner's 4 week programme covering everything they were struggling with – and I recorded and had it on sale within 3 days.

Yes, you read that right. It was hard work but I did it and I only marketed it for 2 weeks. I sold 35 places. So I had spare money to keep me going after the holiday. Bonus. And I had 35 new happy customers who got a bargain programme, many of whom went on to spend a lot more with me.

YOUR CUSTOMERS ARE NOT MIND READERS

Your existing customers are the most likely to buy from you because they already know you, like you, trust you and are happy (hopefully) with their purchase. You don't have to start relationship building from scratch as you would with new customers. Always look to your existing customers first when you want to grow your business because they are your best source of additional income.

Do your existing customers know about everything you sell? Have you told them? Or are you expecting them to be mind readers?

Just checking, because it's often the case that your customers are buying things from other people that they could buy from you, simply because they don't know you sell them.

> If you sell a range of products or services you will probably find that the same customers buy the same things, time and time again and yet you could be selling so much more to them.

HOW CAN YOU LET THEM KNOW?

Here are some ideas:

- Send out an email saying ' did you know we do this?' with some of your top selling (and not so well known) products showcased in all their glory.

- Send out a regular e-newsletter, once a month, and each month showcase one or two products or services. Talk about the difference they are making, the results they are getting and even include mini case studies. Also include lots of additional value through tips, trade secrets and 'how to' sections.

- Showcase your products and services regularly on social media – again, highlight the VALUE they add rather than just telling people what they are. Why should people care?

 Add a little note onto their invoice saying – I know you buy this regularly, but did you know we also do this?

- Use the Amazon approach – when you put an item in your basket on Amazon, it always says 'people who bought that also bought THIS' and gives you suggestions of additional purchases based upon what other people have bought. How can you do the same? It might mean tailored emails to purchasers of certain products or if you can, see if you can offer a similar function on your website. It's proven to increase sales.

- Drop your best customers a postcard offering them money off a different product or service to what they usually buy, or a free taster to get them to try it.

- Ring your top customers and ask what else you can do for them. Ask them what else they need that they can't currently find, and see if it's something you could easily provide within your existing business.

- Do a survey and list ALL your products/services then ask people to tick what they have bought from you – they will have to read through the whole list to see which they have bought. Also ask them what else you could provide for them. Offer an incentive to get people to complete it. Promote it far and wide for at least 2 weeks and aim to get as many responses from 'good fit' people as possible. Tailor the prize to attract the 'right' people rather than just freebie hunters.

HOW CAN I ATTRACT NEW CUSTOMERS?

What sort of new customers do you want to attract? Not all new customers are good customers – I'm guessing you're a bit more choosy and you'd actually like to attract lovely new customers who think you're amazing and keep buying more, while sending all their friends your way too? Hmm, thought so, me too.

So, remember in the introduction (you did read the introduction didn't you?) where I talked about Super Customers? This is where it all starts coming together.

The Super Customer approach is based on the fact that you're a micro business owner – you have limited time, money and energy to spend on marketing because you've got a business to run and kids to bring up and you sometimes need to sleep.

You can't market to everyone so you may as well market to the people who are most likely to buy, right? Obviously! Why wouldn't you do this?
So, in answer to 'how can I attract new customers?' I would say - how can I attract new Super Customers and you'll have more success and sell more in the process.

There's a section on marketing and social media in this book that will give you loads of tips, hints and techniques to get your marketing working a treat – read that. But also, look at what you could put together NOW to get new interest and new customers.

When you're deciding what to do, think about what your Super Customers really need right now. What are they struggling with? What would they give their eye teeth to get their hands on?

HOW IT WORKS FOR ME

In my business, I know my Super Customers are struggling with marketing ideas, with pricing, with selling, with getting more customers, with finding more time in the day. They feel stuck and frustrated and broke.

So, if I needed to drive sales quickly and attract new business I would put together some 30-60 minute masterclass videos that they can watch in their own time and that are very affordable but PACKED with value, on selling for scaredy-cats, on getting more done, on how to price like a pro – you get the idea. And it would work. Because I am giving my fans and subscribers what they need and want.

WHAT COULD YOU PUT TOGETHER?

Deals and Bundles

What irresistible deal or bundle could you put together to entice new customers into your business? What would your Super Customers LOVE? What products are always popular and how can you make them more accessible and affordable to tempt people in? What can you add that costs you very little but makes the deal so much sweeter? Get your thinking cap on!

Seasonal Offers

What deals and offers are particularly relevant right now? What seasonal events can you tap into? Are YOUR Super Customers struggling with school holidays and can you help them? What do they need? What do they WANT? What can you tie in to summer, Halloween, Christmas, Easter, football season, Wimbledon, the Olympics? How can you tap into the mood of the moment and get new customers to find you and buy from you? Think!

Tasters

Can you put together an easy 'in' without any long-term commitment or big financial outlay? Can you make it really easy for people to buy? Can you put sample packs together? Offer a 'lite' trial service? Can you let people experience what you sell in a way that's really easy for you and will give them a true taste, so the right people go on to buy more? Can you offer short intro sessions? A really affordable starter class? Despite what you might think, free offers and trial aren't always a good idea because people generally don't value free. Your Super Customers will be happy to invest a little bit to make sure that what you sell is for them.

A Super Sale

If you're in the UK you'll be familiar with the clothing and homewares chain 'NEXT'. They have legendary sales a few times a year – they email out invitations for you to book your ON-LINE shopping slot, they open the doors to the stores at 5am and there is ALWAYS a queue! It's crazy! And do you know what's crazier? The story goes that they buy in certain stock JUST FOR THE SALES (I'm sure they sell it at a couple of stores at a higher price to comply with retail law...) Now if that's true then it's genius because it guarantees they always have tons of items available for shoppers, who are in true 'shop till you drop' sale-shopping mood and their sales make up a HUGE part of their income each year. They have become a tradition.

My question to you is 'how can you use that idea in your business'?
Can you buy in stock at a good price and sell it on to attract new customers and sales? Even if you only really intend to sell your own stuff, can you drive sales by offering lovely things that someone else has made, at a good price and a good profit? After all, the goal is to bring in some cash, attract new customers and get them onto your site or into your shop to buy more, but you have to tempt them in first and if it's not feasible to heavily discount your own stuff, this might be a way around it.

EARLY BIRD OFFERS

Can you tell your email subscribers and existing customers about a product that is coming soon? I use this approach in my business, I call it the 'Sell Then Build' approach. In my case I will come up with an idea for a coaching programme and I'll scope it out as if I was going to build it. Then I tell my tribe that it's coming, offer them an amazing Early Bird Deal that's usually better than half price and see if people buy. If they do, then I know I've hit the spot and I get building. If no-one buys I know it's not quite right and I either ditch it for now or tweak it and put it out again a few weeks later.

The Early Bird deal means that they might be waiting for a month or 6 weeks for the programme to become available but they have got it at the best price ever, so they are happy to wait.

From my perspective it proves to me that people will buy AND it brings me in some cash while I build the product, which is all scoped out and ready to record.

How can you use Early Bird offers in your business? Lots of people do it with events and activities, where they offer an Early Bird price for early booking. They get cash in before the even and the customer gets a great deal. What could YOU do with an Early Bird offer? Thinking cap time!

SCHOOL HOLIDAY SOCIAL MEDIA TIPS

Social media sites such as Facebook, Twitter and Linked in are great marketing tools but it is SO easy to waste time on non-productive social media activities, to get sucked into the vortex that is Facebook or Twitter and look up an hour later, wondering what you've actually accomplished! This is the LAST thing you need in the school holidays when time is at a premium.

You need to make sure that any time you spend on social media is time well spent. It's about:

- Attracting Super Customers
- Giving value and showing you're an expert
- Building your profile
- Helping you stay top of mind
- Building your list
- Building relationships
- Showcasing your products and services

FACEBOOK

If your Super Customers are on Facebook, here are some tips to help you get the best from it:

- Talk to your Super Customers – don't try to please everyone. It will make your Facebook marketing quicker and easier and you need all the help you can get in the school holidays when time is short.

- Be yourself, let your personality shine through – don't waste time trying to sound more 'professional'.

- Share great value information your Super Customers will love, and they will keep coming back – share your expertise.

- Fill out your about section – include a link to your website and make it easy to see who your page is for and how you help them. Mine says 'I help women build brilliant businesses'.

- Use Video – it's great for building relationships and getting reach!

- Don't get hung up on 'likes' – remember every 'like' is an individual – you want to attract individuals who love what you do rather the collect meaningless 'likes'

- Use the 'insights' section to see when your fans are online and where they are from, so you can tailor what and when you post.

- Use the built-in 'Schedule' function to schedule posts in advance – one less thing to worry about in the school holidays!

- Try using the 'Boost Post' paid feature to promote any particularly important posts – especially your irresistible freebie to help build your list

- Ask questions – make them questions your page fans can't get wrong. I ask things like' how did you come up with your business name', or 'what's the best piece of advice you've ever been given' or 'where in the world are you' – they always get good engagement

---

 The Girls Mean Business
Published by Claire Mitchell [?] · July 17 at 7:25pm · Edited · ☀

Did you turn your hobby into a business? What was the biggest change you had to make? Mindset? Pricing?Structure?

Love, Claire xx

- Remember it takes time and work to build a good fan-base on Facebook – likes are cheap but engagement comes when you spend time finding out what your page fans want and how you can help them

- Share quandaries – I do this with 'reader questions' on my page. I often get ladies messaging my page with questions and rather than answer them privately, I check that they're ok for me to share them on my page and I ask my page fans to answer. Many heads are better than one and people love to help – the person gets her question answered, lots of ladies share their knowledge and feel like they have helped and my page gets lots of activity.

 The Girls Mean Business
Published by Claire Mitchell [?] · June 4 · ☀

Reader Question from Lisa: "When you are having quiet periods what can you do go still hit your sales targets? I have a shop and things like weather can have a massive impact on my business.

So I can look at my last few years figures and roughly base my takings around them and then the weather is shocking and your sales plummet. Sales are not a good idea as they de value the product and customers start waiting for sales to shop. Thanks xx"

Come on, girls! Let's get our thinking caps on and share some ideas!

Love, Claire xx

- Quotes work really well on social media – pop over to www.brainy-quotes.com or www.goodreads.com/quotes and pick quotes you love. Remember to credit the person who said the quote you're using, don't ever pretend you've thought it up – not cool AND you'll get caught out

"Lack of direction, not lack of time, is the problem. We all have twenty-four hour days."
Zig Ziglar

"Instead of wondering when your next vacation is, maybe you should set up a life you don't need to escape from."
Seth Godin

"A woman is like a tea bag; you never know how strong it is until it's in hot water."
Eleanor Roosevelt

"Real integrity is doing the right thing, knowing that nobody's going to know whether you did it or not."
Oprah Winfrey

"Change almost never fails because it's too early. It almost always fails because it's too late."
Seth Godin

"You don't have to be great to start, but you have to start to be great"
Zig Ziglar

"Do one thing every day that scares you."
Eleanor Roosevelt

"The secret to being wrong isn't to avoid being wrong! The secret is being willing to be wrong. The secret is realizing that wrong isn't fatal."
Seth Godin

"Well-behaved women seldom make history."
Laurel Thatcher Ulrich

"No one can make you feel inferior without your consent."
Eleanor Roosevelt

"The biggest adventure you can ever take is to live the life of your dreams."
Oprah Winfrey

- Create MEMES – little images with quotes over them. They are very sharable and easy to make using Canva or PicMonkey AND you can take photos on your phone when you're out and about with the kids to use as backgrounds

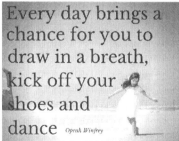

- Record videos when you're out and about on your phone or tablet – a video made on a beach, sharing information your Super Customers will love will be a hit!

- Respond to questions and comments on your posts – this is the sort of thing you can do in the car while you're waiting for the kids to come out of the skate park or dance class

- Share 'behind the scenes' secrets, take photos of your workroom, studio or office

- Share your favourite tools or equipment

- Do a book review

- Review a piece of software or equipment your Super Customers will find interesting

- The same rules apply for social media as they do for traditional networking: build relationships, help others and give value

- PULL in buyers with compelling messages that speak to them and resonate with them – don't just shout!

- You don't attract customers FROM social media. You attract customers THROUGH social media. It's the connections you make and the long-term value you provide those individuals that cultivate the relationship and as a result, they see you as a great person to do business with.

- Get clear on what you want from Social Media. What's your objective? Is it to generate enquiries? Sell? Get people to sign up to your newsletter? Attract more clients? Find referrers or partners? Test your brand or new product ideas?

- It's not about you, it's about them – your Super Customers. What do they want from you? What will make you stand out from the crowd in their eyes? In all of your marketing you ought to be writing with them in mind and social media is no different. Give them relevant, helpful information and content that is of value to them – with no catch, and no expectation.

- Set limits on your time when you're on social media sites – before you know it you've spent hours on Facebook and Twitter without adding people to your database or creating meaningful dialogue, and you've not done any "real" work. Plan your social media time – allow yourself 10 minutes a day, or 30 minutes a couple of times a week and be clear on what you want to achieve in that time. Be consistent and persistent and it will pay off

- Join relevant groups but DON'T go in there and sell, sell, sell. That's just spammy and you'll lose friends and get kicked out! Instead, build relationships, help others and give value. You'll make some great contacts that way.

TWITTER

- Figure out which #hashtags are right for your industry and your Super Customers – search for your key words in the search bar and see what hashtags show up

- Use your top #hashtags to make sure YOUR posts show up in searches for your key terms

#socialmedia #marketing #business #entrepreneur #yougettheidea

- Position yourself as an expert – share your blogs and articles

- Look at trending topics and see if you can add to the discussion

- Use Twitter for PR – make a shortlist of the key magazines, newspapers, websites, radio and TV stations where you'd love to be featured and find the journalists or editors who cover your topic. They will all have a Twitter handle like this @clairemitchell and you can follow them, help them and build a relationship with them. You'll be the first to know if they post a PR opportunity that is perfect for you.

- Share valuable advice and tips your Super Customers will love

- Share photos of work in progress, events you're attending, great finds when you're out and about

- If your Super Customers need to keep up to speed on legal/professional changes, be the person who shares them

- Share inspirational memes

- Summarise key developments and changes in your industry and translate them in a way your Super Customers can easily understand – let them know in practical terms how they can apply them

- Give referrals via Twitter. What goes around comes around.

- Spread your tweets throughout the day, rather than posting the all at once, as people check Twitter at different times of the day.

- Include your Twitter handle your email signature and even on your business cards

- Post discounts and offers on Twitter.

- Find Twitter Hours where your Super Customers hang out – you'll make useful contacts that could turn into suppliers, customers and sub-contractors

#JobHour	10am to 11am	or find vacancies.
#LedburyHour	11am to 12pm	Promoting Ledbury businesses. Join us every Monday
#UKBizLunch	12pm to 1pm	Tweeting while you're eating! A great way to be productive through lunch
#HerefordHour	1pm to 2pm	Our Hereford, open to everyone, a rural city that has so much to offer. Tweet about your business.
#BizHour	2pm to 3pm	Daily general networking event for all types of businesses.
#SouthWestHour	2pm to 3pm	Twitter networking group for the Southwest of England. Repeated again on Thursday.
#B2BHour	3pm to 4pm	Another general networking event. Chance to shout out your business.
#FollowHour	3pm to 4pm	Looking for more followers? Monday to Friday from 3pm to 4pm
#CumbriaHour	7pm to 8pm	Networking for the Lake District
#DarloBizHour	7pm to 8pm	Popular networking hour for businesses in Darlington. (Also #DarloBiz all day every day)

- Use a GOOD headshot, not your wedding photo or a 10 year old image – invest in a professional (but not stuffy) photo you can use on all your Social Media platforms

- Be yourself

- Make sure you complete your profile properly. You never know where you're going to be found first. If someone finds you on Twitter first, make sure they can see what you do and for whom – include your website url too

- Follow your local newpaper editor, your local business club and any industry specific experts and organisations . or journalists you admire. What type of Tweets do you respond to best?

- If people follow you and they look interesting, follow them back!

- Retweet (share) tweets you think your Super Customers will love

- Make sure it's not all about you.

- Shorten your links with a link shortener like www.bitly.com to save on characters – you only have 141 to play with

- Talk to people directly by using @theirname. You'll be surprised by the depth of relationships you can create here.

- Set up lists to help you keep track of key people and organisations – industry experts, trade bodies, social media experts, etc.

- Recommend others you rate and share why. Twitter is a trusted referral engine. Recommend suppliers, clients and anyone else you think deserves it

INSTAGRAM

Instagram works best if you share posts on your expert topic – it's not really about showing what you had for lunch, unless you're a food or health expert. Your followers will follow you because they want to see you sharing your expertise.

- Fill Out Your "Bio" Section - Make sure you fill out the "Bio" section of your Instagram profile. Remember, you never know where some-one will find you first, so make sure you give the right impression and show what you do and whom you help.

- You can't schedule Instagram posts (there are some paid apps that let you do it but they come and go) so make the most of your out and about time during the school holidays. Take photos, make videos and use apps on your phone to turn them into fabulous Instagram posts on the go

- Scroll through your Instagram time-line and see what catches your atten-tion – see what sort of images really pop and stand out. Then aim to make your posts as good as, or better than those

- See how you could use 15 second videos – that's the maximum length of an Instagram video. I've seen fit-ness moves, quick 'how to' videos and montages of artists' work all done bril-liantly in 15 seconds. Use your imagi-nation!

- Take GREAT pictures on your phone. There are lots of apps to help you make your photos look better, add funky frames and overlay words on your photos. Canva and PicMonkey also do this.

- Use Instagram's built-in filters and effects. Instagram has loads of automatic image filters, some are better than others. Have a play, see how they look!

- Make A Collage. Collages of pictures combined into a single image allow you to share more content with each upload. Use an app or Canva to quickly and easily make a collage.

- Add Text to Your Pictures. An image with a quote or text over it is called a MEME – they work brilliantly on all social media including Instagram. Canva, PicMonkey and editing apps make this easy peasy.

- Show people 'behind the scenes'. Your Super Customers will love sneak peeks at how you work.

- Showcase your products and services. Show work in progress, finished pieces, details – if you're a maker, your fans will LOVE to see your work.

- Introduce the team!

- Use #hashtags. These work brilliantly on Instagram. As with Twitter, see which hashtags are most suited to your business and your industry and use them in your posts. Instagram users use hashtags to follow topics they are interested in so figure out what hashtags YOUR Super Customers are searching for and make sure you include them in your posts.

- Share your Instagram Pics on Other Social Networks – you have to be careful cross sharing content across different Social Media platforms because it doesn't always work well but sharing Instagram posts on Facebook and Twitter works great.

- Host an Instagram Contest - see how other people are using them in their business and learn from them.

- See when most of the activity takes place in YOUR Instagram feed – ideally you'll be following lots of people your Super Customers will also be following. Work out when it gets busier and livelier and post more of your content then.

PINTEREST

Pinterest, like Instagram is a visual Social Media platform so you need to find great images to share. Think about what your Super Customers would find useful and interesting. My business is all about teaching and information, I don't have any pretty products to show but I make the most of my content. I create an attractive image to go with every blog or piece of content and I share my best stuff on boards. How can YOU use it?

- Set up boards around topics, types of product, colours – whatever looks best. Don't cram everything onto ONE board

- Name your boards strategically - they will show up in Google searches so think about what your Super Customers are searching for on Google.

- See which posts grab YOUR attention – what catches your eye? What type of images really stand out and look great and how can you emulate them?

- Use Canva or PicMonkey to add text to images – this works well if you are using them to share blog posts (see my boards to see this in action)

- If you are putting product images on Pinterest, make them the best they can be. Try to get the lighting right even if you can't afford professional photos. Bad photos will stand out a mile on Pinterest for all the wrong reasons

- When you are out and about in the school holidays, look around you and see what would make a GREAT image for Pinterest, either as a background for an inspirational quote or just because it fits with your brand – always have your phone camera handy and use editing/photo apps to make your images zing

- Brand your pins – they might get shared far and wide so make sure you put your web address or logo on them so people can find their way back to you

- Share other people's pins your crowd will love, create a board of other people's work you love

- Put prices on product photos – people are much more likely to make a snap buying decision if they can see at a glance how much something they have pinned costs

- Add your website to each pin – go back in and edit each pin after you've uploaded it, add a description that will help it show up in Google searches and add your website

- If you're sharing blog images, link back to the individual blog post, not just your website front page and add a sign-up box to the bottom of each blog post to encourage people to join your mailing list

- Categorise each board – as you create it, it will ask you which category you want it to feature in, this helps you get found

- Follow other people who inspire and interest you, learn from others

- Pin like you mean it – there are lots of abandoned Pinterest boards out there in the Pinosphere, don't let yours be one. The more Pins you share, the more followers you'll get, the more engagement you'll get and the more traffic you'll drive through to your website where people can buy

- Make sure your images are the right size – use the free templates in www.canva.com to get it right

- Make your website pin-friendly – use Pinterest's widget to add a pin-it button to your site

- Can you share valuable teaching information on Pinterest? Think about what your Super Customers would love to know and share it!

LINKEDIN

LinkedIn is the perfect Social Media platform if your Super Customers are in the corporate or professional services world. Also, LinkedIn is amazingly well optimised on Google, and your LinkedIn profile will often appear in Google searches before your own website.

Definitely fill out your profile because, as I've said before, you never know where someone will find you first and you need to make the right first impression.

- Tailor your public profile so it looks like this uk.linkedin.com/in/clairemitchelluk rather than a random bunch of numbers. Go to your account and it will ask you to create a custom URL – that's what you need.

- Add a background photo to your profile, it looks nice and will let you show off your branding or lovely products too! Click Profile >> Edit Profile in LinkedIn's top navigation, then click Add a background photo at the top of your page. Go for 1400 x 425 pixels for the best look and it needs to be under 8 MB.

- Use the words your Super Customers are searching for on Google in your profile so you show up in searches

- LinkedIn lets you add images, videos, presentations and links so USE them! Show off your work, share your keynote presentations and talks, include videos of you demonstrating your art, sharing your knowledge and doing your thing. This is your chance to show you're an expert.

- LinkedIn asks users to endorse other users when they log in – it will suggest people and the skills they think match them. You can choose the skills you think fit that person. If you don't like the skills it is putting forward for you, you can choose better ones

- Recommendations are a great relationship builder. Give recommendations to people who have done great work for you – give them freely and without expectation they will return the favour. Your suppliers will be delighted and it will create lovely goodwill.

- Don't hassle people to give you introductions. Often people will connect to people they don't really know, so asking for an introduction can make it awkward. Better to see if you can connect with that person yourself and see how you can help them.

- Join groups where your Super Customers hang out – don't join to then spam the group with sales messages though (as if you would!). Instead, ask questions, answer questions, add value, help others and share your expert knowledge. This is how great relationships begin.

- If your Super Customers ARE on LinkedIn it's worth setting up and optimising your Company page – it will help you get found and lets you set up sub-pages to showcase products and services.

- Share your Twitter updates on LinkedIn, especially if you share your blogs on there. Even better, if you've scheduled your Tweets to go out over the holidays, it will mean your LinkedIn status gets regularly updated, too.

THINK LIKE A BUSINESS OWNER

So, do you feel like a business owner? Hmm?

Or do you spend most of your time feeling like a cross between a fire-fighter, referee and juggler, struggling to keep everything running if not smoothly, at least so everyone is safe, fed and watered? Congratulations, you just passed the business mum quality standard!

Doing the best you can with what you have is DEFINITELY the only way when you're running a business and you've got little ones – and it reaches another level come the school holidays.

However much you feel like you're clinging on by your fingernails, there are times when thinking like a business owner can really help your business and save you loads of time and energy. It stops you making bad decisions, it stops you being treated like a doormat and being walked over and it helps you to get clear on what you really need to do for your business.

Thinking like a business owner means ignoring the mind monkeys, getting clear on what you want from your business, putting boundaries in place, saying no, pricing properly, ditching the guilt, getting stuff finished and having confidence in yourself and your business.

MIND MONKEYS

As if running a business and looking after children isn't enough, we've also got pesky mind monkeys to contend with. They are the little voices in your head saying "you're not clever enough", "you're not good enough", "nobody will ever pay that", YOU'RE A BAD MUM". Does this sound familiar?

Luckily, they are nothing to worry about.

My take on them is that they are spouting stuff from your past that is stored there to keep you 'safe' and whenever you do something scary like stepping out of your comfort zone, the mind monkeys appear and remind you that scary stuff can get you into trouble.

YOUR PAST DEFINITELY DOES NOT DEFINE YOUR FUTURE!

Don't listen to the mind monkeys!

Actually, mind monkeys are a good sign because they mean you are stretching yourself and doing exactly what they don't want, stepping out of your comfort zone.

You can't grow a successful business without stepping out of your comfort zone so ignore the monkeys and keep going!

WHAT ARE YOU AIMING FOR?

I want you to get really clear on what you want from your business, long term AND in the next 12 months.

- What do you want?
- How many hours do you want to work?
- What sort of people would you love to work with and sell to?
- Do you want business premises?
- Do you want to win awards? Make a difference? Change the world?
- How much money do you want to make? By when?
- What will you do with it? Pay off debt? Have holidays? Buy property? Give to Charity?
- How many products or services will you need to sell to hit that income target?
- Will your current pricing support that? Can you sell enough at your current rates or is it pie in the sky? Do you need to change your pricing model?

If you get clear on this vision for your business now, you can make decisions that will take you in the right direction. You won't get tempted and led astray by BSOs (Bright Shiny Objects) and you'll get to where you want to be so much quicker.

BSOS (BRIGHT SHINY OBJECTS)

Definition: Money making opportunities that fly past you at speed, or twinkle out of the corner of your eye, tempting you to grab them with both hands!

OK, face facts. You're an entrepreneur, you can spot money-making opportunities around every corner and while this is great, it's also a colossal distraction. Entrepreneurs LOVE 'new' so BSOs are very tempting.

The key to dealing with BSOs is to do nothing.

To wait. For a week. Eek! "But, the opportunity might disappear!" You squeal, "I might be too late!". And yes, you might – but if it is meant for you, it will still be there when you've let it lie for a few days. Let the initial buzz wear off, take off the rose-tinted glasses and look at it objectively.

Look at the numbers, look at how much time and energy it's going to take out of your current business and think about what you could do in your current business, if you channelled all that excitement and energy into there instead.

WHERE ARE YOUR BOUNDARIES?

You and I are micro-business owners, we don't have a big team of support staff – we do most things ourselves.

When you don't have boundaries in place in your business, you start getting taken advantage of and that's something you can ill afford at any time, let alone during the school holidays.

What does that look like?
- Customers or clients will start to contact you at stupid hours, like 11 o'clock at night and expect a response
- Some get nasty because they've emailed you on a weekend and haven't had a reply within 10 minutes.
- Customers are friending you on Facebook and personal messaging you while you're out with your family.
- You get people turning up at your house to discuss business when you haven't invited them

None of them sound like great situations to find yourself in, do they?

The thing is, Only YOU can stop it.
- You are allowing this behaviour.
- You are allowing people to treat you like garbage
- By not telling them NOT to do it, you are allowing it
- If you respond to a text at 10.45pm you are basically saying "I'm available"
- If you reply to the email whilst you're on holiday, you are saying "I know I'm supposed to be out of bounds but actually I'm around! Keep talking!"

So, naturally your clients and customers will take advantage of that. If you give them an inch they will take a mile. That's human nature.

If you let them do it then they will do it. The first thing you need to do is stop allowing it.

BOUNDARY TIPS

1. GET CLEAR YOURSELF ON YOUR BOUNDARIES

- What are you going to allow, and what are you not going to allow?
- Are you on holiday and out of bounds or not?
- At what point do you switch off?
- At what point do you stop answering emails, texts and things of an evening?
- Do you work weekends or not?
- Stick to your boundaries because they will immediately give you some freedom - you won't feel tied to the business.
- Even if you love your business now, clients overstepping boundaries is a really quick way to make you start resenting your business

You need to get really clear on what your boundaries are, realising that you need to have time for you, your family and other stuff that you want to do.

2. DECLARE YOUR BOUNDARIES

Once you know what those boundaries need to be you need to tell people about them.

Put your terms of business and your boundaries on your Facebook page, on your website, on an email auto responder.

If you tell people you've got a 48hr response time to emails, you've got a 48hr response time to emails, people aren't going to expect an email from you immediately, they realise it might take some time.

3. STOP FRETTING!

Get rid of that nagging fear that your customers are going to hate you, be annoyed with you, not come back and you're going to lose orders. **I understand! It's a really scary thing to do, but do you want a life or not?** Do you want to be at the beck and call of people who are just taking advantage of you? It's very rare that something is so urgent it needs an answer right now.

Your Super Customers won't mind. They'll be understanding of the fact that you have boundaries.

4. GET USED TO SAYING NO

When you get used to this, it will be a revelation. It will be easier for you to set and stick to your boundaries but you'll also not get guilt-tripped into doing things you don't want to do (be treasurer of the Parent Teacher Association, make cakes for the school raffle, whatever your weakness is).

Take back control of your time. Stop saying yes to things you don't want to do.

Say *'no, I'm sorry I can't'* then shut up. You do not have to justify saying no.

No explanation required. If they pressure you for more information just repeat "I just can't, I'm afraid."

Practise saying it. It works like magic. This works for needy customers who are taking the mickey. It works on people trying to get you to do stuff during the day because you 'work from home'. The more you say it, the better you will feel and the more time you will have to do the things you DO want to do – especially in the school holidays.

GET IT FINISHED, NOT PERFECT!

Perfection is relative. Your idea of perfect is different to mine and you are much more critical of your own work than anyone else will be.

I'm pretty sure I wouldn't notice if one stitch is wonky or one bead isn't quite the same colour. I think what we forget is that because it's so close to us and we are so engrossed in our work all the time, we have this really false idea of perfection

The trouble with getting things perfect, is that 'perfect' never comes and you don't finish them.

- They never get signed off, they never get completed and when they're not finished you can't make any money from them.
- You can't sell a piece of jewellery that YOU don't think is perfect, even if nobody else would ever notice
- You can't put out a webinar if you don't think it's perfect and if you're not prepared to let it go.
- You can't make money unless you ditch that perfectionist streak, let things go and realise that it is totally subjective.

Most of it is in your head and if you're aiming for perfection, what you DO come up with will be easily more than good enough for your clients.

What are you putting off because you are waiting for it to be perfect?

Are you waiting for the perfect time or the perfect outcome?

I guarantee that that's not going to happen, so whatever it is that you're putting off or not finishing, I need you to finish it, it's time now.

Stop letting this thought of false perfection ruin your life and rule your business. It's time to let it go, it's time to get it finished...not perfect and I can't wait to see what comes out of this. Once you ditch that perfectionist streak, amazing things start to happen!

DITCHING THE 'BUSINESS OWNER MUM' GUILT

School holidays are always a challenge when you're a business-owner mum.

You try to get a balance but there are days you'd rather spend with the children, but NEED to get work done – out come the Guilt mind monkeys.

There are days when you'd love to be one of those earth-mother types but to be honest, you have totally had enough of the fighting this week and if you don't get them into childcare, they might find you hiding in the ice-cream freezer at Tesco. And then you feel guilty for NOT wanting to be with your children.

This doesn't only happen in the school holidays but the lack of time, need to get work done while the kids are off and inevitable 'school holiday fatigue' mean that the Guilt mind monkeys feel like gorillas, beating you with the BAD MOTHER stick (been there, got the T-shirt).

- You feel guilty about working when the children are around.
- You feel guilty about NOT working because the children are around.
- You feel guilty for 'farming them out' while you work.
- You feel guilty for sitting working while they are playing.
- You feel guilty saying 'no' when you're working.
- You feel guilty taking time out to be with them when you have work to do

Let me tell you about GUILT

- Guilt does not help anybody
- Guilt does not change the outcome
- Guilt doesn't help your children
- Guilt doesn't make you more productive
- Guilt doesn't make you anything apart from ill

Guilt is a pretty useless emotion, really, same as worry. There is NOTHING to be gained by feeling guilty. So, just stop it? Ok?

There are LOADS of ways to feel guilty, take your pick! I've suffered from all the above many times.

The way to deal with Guilt mind monkeys is to say to yourself, as often as you need:

"I am doing the best I can with what I have. I am a GOOD mum".

It's my mantra. It sometimes feels like a tiny shield against a huge Guilt gorilla, but the more I say it, the better I feel.

Here are some more to chew on while you're at it!

- You are a brilliant mum.
- You are running your business to make life better for your family.
- You are working stupid hours to bring in some extra money for holidays or treats, things your family couldn't otherwise have
- You are not taking the easy route – you COULD take a job working for someone else but then you couldn't be there much at all during school holidays.
- Being a business owner means you can be around for your children. Maybe not every day because you need to keep the business going, but more than if you worked for someone else full time
- You are ALLOWED to have a business!
- You are ALLOWED to channel your creativity and have this business rather than give in to the rat race

You get the idea. Whatever those Guilt mind monkeys are saying, you need a come-back mantra to send them packing.

Guilt is so unproductive, it's such a nasty insidious thing that creeps in and makes you feel bad when actually you were pootling along fine – snap out of it.

Don't lose precious time feeling guilty – enjoy the moment, get stuck into whatever you are doing and make the most of it, from time with the children to time in the business – don't let the Guilt mind monkeys spoil what would otherwise be a lovely day.

LITTLE OLD ME

Thinking like a business owner can feel tricky when you've been used to thinking like 'little old me'.

'Little old me' is a pushover. She doesn't stand up for herself. She doesn't dare charge proper prices because she's not good enough and anyway, no-one would pay that anyway.

Little old me needs to go! You are better than that. You are a business owner, so start thinking like one!

How This Works:

LITTLE OLD ME

She is scared of facing facts. She doesn't know her numbers because it's too scary to contemplate and she's always been bad at maths. When she priced her products or services, she looked at what everyone else was charging and decided where she fit in the pecking order (and it wasn't at the top). She isn't sure, but she doesn't think she's making much money…

BUSINESS OWNER ME

She is awesome. She knows all the cost in her business, in fact she knows how much it costs her to make each product or deliver each service. She prices properly and makes a great profit. She doesn't compete on price, she knows her value to her Super Customers and she only markets to them. She's become a bit of a star in her field, the 'go to' person if you want the best – people know they will pay more but it's worth it.

The only difference between Little Old Me and Business Owner Me is CONFIDENCE.

Which means, you can become Business Owner Me right now. Go on! Confidence is all in your head and only you can flip that switch. You have to decide to be confident. So do it!

What's the worst that can happen?

Someone laughs at you. So what?

Someone says 'I could make that myself for half the price!'
So what? They are NOT your Super Customer

You get it wrong. So what? We all make mistakes, I reckon I've made hundreds along the way and some of them were BIG. But I'm still here and you will be too.

Nobody buys. OK that's easy. It's either wrong people, wrong products or you're not showing the value. Get really clear on your Super Customer, understand what they want and need and make sure your marketing targets them, and shows them why your business is a brilliant fit. I've shown you how in this book.

Competitors keep undercutting you or copying you. So what? Let them get on. They can only survive for so long that way. You're NOT competing on price, you are attracting customers because of the VALUE you add – they are not. If they are copying, they can only go so far. Your products and services are unique to YOU because YOU are the magic ingredient. Your business has YOUR energy, YOUR passion, YOUR experience, expertise and knowledge behind it. It might be hugely annoying (I know, I've had it happen to me) but if you spend your time and energy worrying about them and feeling bitter, you're not putting good energy into your business. MIND YOUR OWN BUSINESS. They will come unstuck eventually I'm sure but you'll be too busy having a brilliant time to notice.

When you decide to be confident it will affect all areas of your business and your life. Some people might not like it, but that's hard luck.

Confidence is what will make your business fly and send 'Little Old Me' packing. It's up to you. Only YOU can decide to be confident and sometimes you have to get your drama on and ACT confident, even if you're quaking in your boots.

Let me tell you something. The more you ACT confident, the MORE CONFIDENT you really become. It's like magic. This is one time when 'fake it till you make it' really works. What's stopping you? Let 'Little Old Me' go, she's had her time – it's YOUR TIME NOW!

WORK FROM ANYWHERE GIRL

This is my alter-ego, especially during school holidays and I highly recommend you try it! Work From Anywhere Girl gets loads done during the school holidays. She can work from the unlikeliest of places and her kids are happy too! Result!

I'm very lucky, I can run my business from anywhere. It's best if I have Wifi but there are always loads of things I can do without it. I don't ever sit waiting somewhere thinking 'darn it, I could have been getting on with….' Because I take my Work From Anywhere Kit with me when I'm out and about, and I pick something and get started.

I've told you about Family Time, Work Time and Combo Time (page 78 if you've not read it) right? Combo time is what I have most of during school holidays. Chloe might be at a dance class, gymnastics session or at soft play – she doesn't need me to be hands on because she's busy, but I need to be there to see to her when she's finished or needs food/drink. I could waste that time waiting around, mindlessly browsing Facebook or watching cat videos but I don't. I worked out a long time ago that I wasted hours this way, so nowadays I do something about it.

I have a bag packed with a notebook and pens, my phone and iPad and maybe even my laptop if I'm going to be at soft play for hours. I stick my iPad charger and laptop charger in too, in case I run out of juice and can find a handy plug socket (our soft play has them available for parents to use). If we're taking the car I stick the whole lot in my favourite flowery Cath Kidston holdall. If we're on the train or walking, I'll stick them (minus the laptop) in a rucksack and off we go.

There are LOADS of jobs you can do while you're out and about and on the go. The goal isn't to spend the WHOLE time working when you could be spending time with your family. The idea is, if everyone is off doing their 'thing' and you're minding the towels or the dog or guarding the picnic, you can still work.

Here are just a few:

BEACH BUSINESS BOOSTERS

Good for...

Photos/VIDS

Listening

Watching

Writing

At the beach? You lucky thing! Well, my advice is to chill out and catch a tan but if you MUST get your business brain into gear, here are some suggestions for you. You have no wifi but you DO have lovely surroundings and even when you're covered in sand and sun cream you should still be able to use a notebook and pen. The BEST use of beach time is to listen so you can keep an eye on the kids and learn at the same time...

1. Download podcasts to your phone before you go, stick in your earphones and dig out your notebook. You can watch the kids from your sun lounger while filling your big brain with brilliant business tips. People will be intrigued when you suddenly sit up, spill your Pina Colada down your bikini, grab your notebook and start scribbling while muttering about marketing...happens every time...

2. Download Awesome Business School or other classes to your phone or tablet and watch videos. You're not going to be able to implement much if you're away in foreign climes so make sure you scribble like a crazy woman and capture all those 'aha!' moments. When you get back, you can make time to start implementing.

3. Take gorgeous photos. There's nothing like a blue sky, the sea, pebbles, waves and other seasidey things to create gorgeous images you can use on your website and social media. These images are perfect for MEMES and will save you buying images or using free images everyone else is using. Get snapping on your phone and stock up on amazing images!

4. Dream. Stretch out in the sun and let your mind wander to how you can develop your business. Dream big. Look at how you would love your business to run; how much money you'd like to make, how many beach holidays you'd love to have each year, who you'd love to have working with you. Dream then scribble THEN when you get back, turn it into a vision board that will inspire you, and fill it full of the photos you took in point 3. If your holidays are anything like mine you'll get at least 10 minutes of dreaming in before a sandy child comes and drips ice lolly down you....

5. Talk to your family. If you're out and about having lovely lunches and dinners, share your dream and plans. Tell them how you're putting everything in place and ask them how if they like the sound of it and they can help you. You might get some unexpected support AND they'll stop asking you what you do all day.

6. Scribble. Ideas for blogs, things you can post on social media, new product ideas. Your brain is usually at its most creative when you're relaxed, especially if you're stuck somewhere you can't do anything about it. That's why I get my best ideas in the shower and while driving - your job is to capture the fab ideas and tackle them when you get home.

7. Record some videos - NO not you in your bikini (unless you want to) but if you're dressed up nicely and you're out and about looking tanned, take 5 minutes to share something your Super Customers would love. Save up your videos and post them over a few weeks when you get back, then watch your FB engagement grow.

8. Read a great book. Not necessarily a business book but maybe an autobiography. I've had some great ideas while reading about how other people have built businesses.

PRODUCTIVE PLANE JOURNEYS

Good for...

Reading ✓

Listening ✓

Watching ✓

Writing ✓

Flights for me are a little hit and miss. Sometimes my 7 year old will get engrossed in her iPad or the on-board movie for hours. Other times I pretty much have to entertain her the whole trip. BUT flights can be a great time to get stuck into business while taking your mind off the crumby in-flight meal and snoring passenger 3 rows down. Here are 9 in-flight business-boosting ideas for you...

1. Download podcasts to your phone before you go, stick in your earphones and dig out your notebook. Let's face it, you're stuck in that seat for the next few hours so you may as well retreat into your own little world of business tycoonism and plan world domination at fifty thousand feet (I have no idea how high a plane flies but that sounds quite high)

2. Download Awesome Business School or other programmes/classes to your phone or tablet and watch videos – scribble like a crazy woman while facing up to the fact that you're not going to be able to put ANY of this into action until you get back. But you can go and enjoy your trip knowing you were building your business while everyone else was watching Nuns On The Run.

3. Come up with ideas for Facebook posts

4. Come up with ideas for Tweets

5. Come up with blog ideas and scope them out – I tend to draw mind maps when I do this

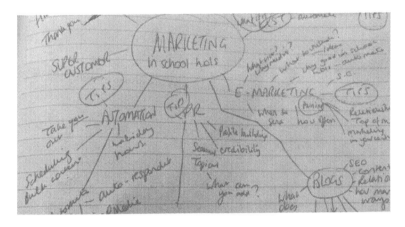

6. Read a brilliant book. Autobiographies are great. Or choose a type of book you've never chosen before – you might surprise yourself

7. Scope out some blogs so all you have to do is fill in the detail when you're home – again mind maps are brilliant for this.

8. Think about your goals and targets. How much do you want to make this year? Next year? How much will you need to sell each month to achieve that? Where are you now? How big is the gap between your goals and your actual sales? Where are the extra sales going to come from? I've got some great podcasts on my website to help you with this so make sure you have a good browse before you leave for your trip.

9. Think about your Super Customer. Get really clear on who they are and why they love you. Start to fill in some details about their life. Think about where they live, how old they are, how they spend their time. Think about what they are struggling with, what issues and problems they have that you can solve and what they are spending their money on at the moment. Figure out where they hang out online and offline. Holidays are a great time to mull over your Super Customer description as it often changes and evolves over a couple of weeks. By the time you get home you'll be a Super Customer marketing ninja and you'll be raring to go.

BUILD YOUR BUSINESS AT THE PARK

good for...

Photos/videos

Listening

Watching

Writing

If you're out and about with the kids at the park or other outdoor play area there are things you can do to keep your business running smoothly - the key thing about the great outdoors is that there is NO WIFI (eek!) so you have to tackle tasks you can do with your phone/tablet and a notebook that don't require the internet. The good news is there is lots you can still do...

1. Download podcasts to your phone before you go, stick in your earphones and dig out your notebook. You can watch the children and still be available for them while having brilliant 'aha!' moments as you learn. If you stick your earphones in you're less likely to attract casual chatters, too. You can take regular play breaks with the kids if you want, then pick up the podcasts where you left off when they decide to go off and play happily without you.

2. Download Awesome Business School or other classes to your phone or tablet and watch videos - make notes as you go and see if you can IMPLE-MENT any at the time. Make a to-do list of things you can put into place once the kids go to bed - if you do this every day or a few times a week you will be amazed at how much you can achieve in just a few weeks. By the time the holidays are over you'll be a business ninja.

3. Take photos for MEMES. The beauty of the great outdoors is that you can take loads of photos to use as background for memes to use on Social Media. I've taken photos of the sky, grass, pebbles, flowers, and walls, anything that will make a nice background to add a quote or inspirational saying onto using an app on my phone or tablet.

4. Record videos on your phone/tablet. Videos work really well on social media as well as being great content for your website. Why not record little 'tips' videos you can share on FB, where you tackle common questions you get asked about your products or services. It doesn't matter about the background noise of the park, just introduce it and say 'I'm at the park and just got a great question on email (or my FB page) and so I decided to make you a quick little video RIGHT NOW to answer it'. These videos work really well and although you might feel a bit weird if passers by wonder what you're doing, your videos will get great reach!

5. Create some MEMES - use some of the fab apps available to create gorgeous images to use on Facebook and Instagram.

6. Come up with blog ideas - scope them out on a mind map so all you have to do when you get home is fill in the gaps

7. Watch the world go by and get inspired - my best blogs come from people watching and from things that have happened to me. Look at ways to incorporate what you're seeing and experiencing into lessons for your customers and clients.

8. Ask your children what you could do to let people know about your business. My 7 year old has come out with some bizarre and very funny suggestions that inspired some of my marketing - seeing what you do through a child's eyes can give you a whole new perspective.

SOFT PLAY BUSINESS BOOSTERS

good for...

Social Media

Listening

Watching

Writing

Yes, I know soft play is basically a room full of screaming children hurling themselves around the room at speed BUT I'm a huge fan of soft play, especially if it has wifi. Team TGMB can be found most Saturday afternoons at our local soft play and we get LOADS done. Here are 14 things you can do if you find a soft play with wifi...

1. Download podcasts to your phone before you go, stick in your earphones and dig out your notebook. You can drown out some of the noise, get really focused and learn loads while still keeping an eye on the children. Soft play areas usually have decent coffee too - bonus!

2. Download Awesome Business School or other classes to your phone or tablet and watch videos - make notes as you go and see if you can IMPLE-MENT any at the time. Make a to-do list of things you can put into place once the kids go to bed - if you do this every day or a few times a week you will be amazed at how much you can achieve in just a few weeks. By the time the holidays are over you'll be a business ninja.

3. Do a brain dump! Then make a list of 10 minute jobs

4. Come up with ideas for Facebook posts

5. Come up with ideas for Tweets

6. Create Pins using photos on your phone or from free sites

7. Come up with MEME ideas – think of sayings and quotes you could use

8. Make MEMES using photos on your phone or from free sites

9. Come up with blog ideas and scope them out

10. Respond to comments on your social media accounts

11. Check your Facebook Insights and see what has worked and what hasn't worked on your Facebook page - do more of what's working

12. Set up a Pinterest board and start pinning images of your work that you've saved to your phone/computer

13. Optimise your Wordpress blog posts using the free YOAST plugin - fill out your keyword info until you turn the traffic light green

14. Optimise your PINS on Pinterest - put a good description on each pin containing keywords you want to be found in a Google search for - link back each pin to your website

So, you can see that Combo time can be really productive. You can get loads of marketing and business-building tasks done while you're out and about with the children, even if you only have a few minutes to spare.
In addition to all these you can make phone calls and write emails, if you need to.

Combo time has been my school holiday saviour – I don't put my business on hold, I just work it in and around my family AND I can tell the Guilt mind monkeys to do one. Win win!

HOLIDAY RULES

When you're running a business with the kids around during school holidays, you have to lighten up, realise you're not going to get as much done as usual and stop stressing – after all, your kids are only young once so you want to try to have some time with them, too. Holiday rules definitely apply.

- Do the best you can with what you have
- Stop beating yourself up
- Don't let anyone guilt-trip you
- Don't guilt-trip yourself
- Understand this is only temporary
- You just need to get by for a few weeks
- Your Super Customers will understand
- It's OK to have time off
- Workarounds are the perfect solution
- Ask for help
- Be realistic
- Don't burn yourself out
- You're awesome
- You can't please everyone
- You're doing this FOR the family
- You're a great mum
- It's only business
- **HAVE FUN!**

I've put together some lovely freebie bonuses for you because you've bought this book. You can download them all here www.bitly.com/sosbizbook

16882151R00096

Printed in Great Britain
by Amazon